They Called It Golf Because Flog Was Already Taken

Frank Fenton
and
David Grimes

Cartoons by Al Konetzni

Pineapple Press, Inc.
Sarasota, Florida

This book is dedicated to my wife, Kathy, who has been tolerant an untold number of hours, days, and years while I pursued my golf education, career, and inventions. And to my two daughters, Karen and Christina, who often wondered where their dad was while they were growing up and I was traveling around the U.S. and the world in pursuit of better golf clubs.
— Frank Fenton

To Michael and Teri, who were too smart to take up the game.
—David Grimes

Inquiries should be addressed to:
Pineapple Press, Inc.
P.O. Box 3889
Sarasota, Florida 34230
www.pineapplepress.com

Library of Congress Cataloging-in-Publication Data
Fenton, Frank, 1953.
    They called it golf because flog was already taken / by Frank Fenton
and David Grimes.—1st ed.
        p. cm.
    ISBN 1–56164–288–6 (pbk. : alk. paper)
1. Golf—Humor. I. Grimes, David. II. Title.
GV967 .F43 2003
796.352—dc21
                                                    2003011539

First Edition
10 9 8 7 6 5 4 3 2 1

Design by Shé Heaton
Printed in the United States of America

"Wait just a minute. I gotta get my nine iron!"

Table of Contents

Frank Fenton

David Grimes

Index 143

1

Lee Trevino

Frank Fenton

I n the summer of 1969, I was sixteen years old and had been playing golf for a little over a year. I had been caddying at my father's golf club outside Washington, D.C., for a few years to pick up a little spending money even before I took up playing the game at fifteen. I was paid the usual $3 to $4 per bag, occasionally getting as much as $5. At those prices I often carried "double," which meant a heavy bag on each shoulder. God help me if the player had one of those pro-size leather bags with a few dozen balls along for the ride. Of course at that age, with several years of trekking over the course and over a year of playing this fine game, I was confident that there was little about golf that I didn't know.

Then it happened—the biggest thing in a young man's life. No, not that. Something far more important and memorable. We were having actual professional PGA Tour players come to our golf course to play a charity exhibition, and I was selected from the dwindling ranks of caddies to carry one of the bags. There were to be only four players: Jim Hiskey, a local pro who had played the Tour in the 1960s; Lee Elder, the well-known

Tour player from the Washington, D.C., area; the newly crowned U.S. Open Champion, Orville Moody; and the previous year's U.S. Open Champion, Lee Trevino. My fellow caddies and I all were anxious to see who got whose bag. We drew lots and darned if I didn't get Trevino. He was already famous, and with a major under his belt and a reputation as a fast-talking, fast-swinging golf hustler from Texas, he was my kind of guy.

The group of young guys that I normally caddied and played with knew every inch of that golf course. We were known as pretty good players, too. So when we gave yardage or advice, we were used to people adhering to what we said. Then I caddied for Lee Trevino. He played shots that I never imagined possible. On the third hole, a medium-length par four, he hit his drive out to within 150 yards of the green. I began to hand him a seven iron as he reached for a four iron. "No, Mr. Trevino." I said. "You're only a hundred and fifty out and there's an out-of-bounds fence just behind the green." "Kid," he said, "let me show you a shot." He then proceeded to hit the most beautiful little knock-down four iron into the front bank of the raised green—and it bounced up to about twelve feet from the hole. He made the putt for birdie. That was the last time I tried to hand him a club before he made up his mind what type of shot he wanted to play.

The next hole was a par five that went up a steep hill, then over water to a small green with a huge oak tree overhanging the right side. Again, there were out-of-bounds stakes nestled tight by the right side of the green. Trevino hit his tee ball into some high weeds off to the right of the fairway. I mean deep stuff, waist high. His ball was actually hanging in this grass, maybe ten inches off the ground. I looked at him and waited for his club selection. You couldn't see the green, water, or OB from where we were standing, and knowing that he had never played this course before, I told him what was up ahead. Surely he would chip out to the fairway and try to hit the green in three. Nope. I just about gagged when he took out a three wood. My God! He wasn't planning on hitting this ball from this hanging lie to the green! He asked me again for the distance (which was such a ridiculous question it was hard for me to calculate, since I had never seen anyone try to hit a ball to that green from that spot). I gave him the yardage and direction and stepped back. "He's gonna really be mad when he sees what he's done," I thought. Lee Trevino then hit one of the most incredible shots I have ever seen any player hit. Ever. And I have seen a lot of shots in person and on television. He took that flat swing of his and hit that ball so solid that it arched up against the sky out to the left of the green and faded back toward the hole. This was impossible. The gallery cheered as the ball landed on the green. I was so awestruck I still, to this day, don't remember what he made on the hole. I think he birdied it, but he may have eagled it.

As the round progressed, Lee and Orville were joking back and forth and at some point Orville thought that it would be funny to take Trevino's putter. He came up to the bag and with his finger to his lips, told me to be quiet as he pilfered Lee's club. He then handed it to some kid who promptly ran away. I knew this was going to be trouble when Lee got to the green and reached for his putter. Orville thought that this was a real hoot. I'm not sure that Lee felt the same way. After sending off some local kids to find the youngster who got Trevino's putter, we finally retrieved it. Trevino told me to keep Moody away from his bag from then on.

Just for fun, Trevino began to show the crowd some of his

old hustling playing techniques. He would putt with his foot as well as most people did with a putter (and this was with a full set of steel spikes on the bottom of the shoes back then). He hit a shot that, at the time, amazed me, but which I later learned was really quite easy to perform. He teed up his ball, covered it completely with a paper cup, and then hit a tremendously long and straight drive, blowing up the cup as if it had been hit by a rifle shot. As I became more knowledgeable about the physics involved in hitting a golf ball, I realized that the wall of the cup (when placed directly against the back of the ball) served the same effect that grass would when you hit a "flyer." The cup wall lessened the ball spin (backspin and sidespin) and caused it to fly farther and straighter. This is why the USGA doesn't let you put "foreign material" on the club face. A great hustler trick!

Trevino still had a reputation as a gambler at that time. One of his most famous methods of play was to tee off with a Dr. Pepper bottle. He actually had a Dr. Pepper sticker on the side of his bag. I assume that he had some kind of endorsement deal with them back then. He would wrap cloth tape around the neck end of the bottle and throw up the ball and swat it down the fairway like hitting a fungo bat. The deposit soda bottles of that era were made of very thick, strong glass. He had me go out in the fairway and popped shots toward me of 100, then 150, then close to 200 yards. This guy could control a golf ball.

When we were finished for the day I carried Lee's clubs up to the clubhouse and thanked him for the privilege of carrying his bag. This was a charity event and the players were not being paid any money that day. The other caddies and I had already been instructed not to charge the players for our work. Lee would hear none of this and tried to give me some money. I said no, thank you. He then stuffed a $20 bill in my shirt pocket and told me to go out and have a good time on him. This was a huge amount of money for what I normally got $4 to do. Plus I got these great stories to tell. I never forgot that act of generosity.

Years later, when I was running golf club research and development at Spalding Sports, I was called to a meeting up in the very formal board room on the second floor at Spalding Worldwide headquarters where I worked. In came Lee Trevino for his first meeting with the folks at Spalding to discuss the details of a possible endorsement contract. In the prim and starched room, with an oil painting of A.G. Spalding himself staring down at us, Lee reviewed one of Spalding's new balls. He was asked if he thought he could play this type of ball. He promptly stuck the ball in his teeth and bit down on it. "Feels okay to me," he said. We hired him.

At the end of that meeting I mentioned to Lee that I had caddied for him some twenty years before. He said he remembered the event, but I think he was just trying to be nice. I worked with Lee for the next several years until I left Spalding. When we had our meetings on new products, it was always more productive to get Lee away from the galleries at the golf tournaments and sit down and talk with him. He was really easy to talk with in person, when he was not "on stage" in front of the crowds. I still see him out on the Senior PGA Tour every now and then and he always has time to stop and say hello.

As we all know, Lee went on to win the U.S. Open again in 1971, as well as the British Open that year and the next and the PGA Championship in 1974 and 1984. Since I only saw Ben Hogan hit balls toward the end of his time, I can't say who was the best ball striker. I saw Lee Trevino hit balls in his prime, and he was remarkable.

2

Driver Fitting

Frank Fenton

n my travels I see all kinds of golfers playing with all types of
equipment. One thing that I've noticed is that too many
golfers play with clubs that are ill-suited for their games. I
see high-handicap players with very low lofted woods and thin,
blade-style irons. It is no wonder that these players tell me they
wish they could carry the ball farther in the air. Most golfers
would benefit from custom-fitting their clubs (at least to some
degree) to help correct any undesirable tendency they may
have. It doesn't have to be a two-hour analysis by a swing guru.
The more you know about your own game and shot patterns,
the easier and quicker this process can be completed.

When I go out to the PGA, Senior PGA, and LPGA Tours, golf
club manufacturers such as Taylor Made, Cleveland Golf and
Callaway, along with shaft suppliers like Aldila and True
Temper, spend time talking with and helping fit the Tour play-

ers. They do this to ascertain the type of shots the player wants to hit or the problem the player needs to fix. If the world's best golfers take the time to determine what clubs and shafts fit them the best, shouldn't you?

Of course you may have different goals than the Tour players. You may just be out trying to have some fun at the game. Even so, you should at least look at a few things that will help make you a better golfer. Obviously, being young, six foot two, strong, and practicing sound fundamentals all day long is the best way to improve your game. If you don't have all these capabilities at your disposal, consider the following tips on choosing the right clubs for you.

There are many details to custom fitting an entire set of clubs, but in this chapter I will touch only on a few of the fine points you should review when selecting a driver. Look for obvious things about your game. If you drive the ball very high and get little distance, then try a lower lofted driver, perhaps with a higher center of gravity (CG). This will bring the trajectory down and increase the roll of the ball. If you hit too low, try the opposite. Get a driver with more loft (I find that most average golfers could really benefit from this) and with a lower CG. It is far better to carry the ball in the air and have it land "hot" and roll, than it is to try to run your drives along the ground out to a playable distance.

In both of these cases you should try out different flex shafts. Most drivers today are fitted with composite graphite shafts because of the strength and lightness of this material. Today, club manufacturers can build overall lighter clubs while still keeping plenty of mass in the business end of the club, the club head. They can also build longer-length drivers with the lighter graphite shafts without the swing weight going up to unreasonable numbers. A longer-length driver can help you hit the ball farther, but be careful not to get one that is too long for your height or arm length. A long-length driver that you cannot swing under control is no good for your game. Try different lengths to be sure that you have the ability to hit fairways from the tee and still get good distance.

Since most male golfers can use either a "regular" or "stiff" flex shaft, I would recommend that you experiment with both to see which one allows you the proper kick and feel to propel the ball a long distance down the fairway. You'll note that I put "regular" and "stiff" in quotes. This is because there are differences between different companies' definitions of what a regular or stiff shaft is. Some companies purposely build their shafts to a softer flex to address the egos of golfers. They may offer a "regular" that is really closer to an "A" (Senior) flex, and a "stiff" that is closer to a normal regular. This is not all bad for many golfers, but you should be aware of it. Also, unless you are a really hard swinger, I would not recommend that you use X-flex (extra stiff) shafts. Even many of the PGA Tour players use stiff rather than X-flex shafts.

Different companies design their drivers with shafts that have more or less torque or a different kick point (we'll discuss both in later chapters). The kick point—sometimes called the flex point—of a shaft, along with the club head loft and CG, will determine the initial launch trajectory of the ball flight. If you need to hit the ball higher, you should try a shaft with a lower kick point, i.e. a shaft that has its main kick point down toward the tip end of the shaft. Conversely, if you want to hit the ball lower you should try a shaft that has its kick point higher, toward the butt end of the shaft. Many players on the LPGA Tour use shafts that have a lower kick point to aid in getting the ball flight up. Many of these women pros use regular flex shafts, but some use stiff. Numerous players on the men's PGA Tour use a higher kick point shaft to keep the ball from ballooning on their tee shots, which they feel gives them more control. Most average male golfers would be better off copying the LPGA player's shaft choice, since their club head speeds are similar.

Lastly, I want to mention the face angle of the driver. The face angle is created by the bore of the hole that the shaft is inserted into. Many golfers slice or fade the ball and should try drivers with closed faces. A closed or hook face is one that, when the club head is viewed from address, looks like it points slightly to the left of the target. This will help slicers. Woods with offset hosels or bent shafts will also help control that slice. A golfer who hooks or draws the ball too much will appreciate a club face that is open (one that looks like it points to the right of the target at address). Don't overlook this feature. It could really help you at impact.

There are other important items to consider such as grip size and type, lie angle, overall weight, swing weight, head shape, and face roll and bulge, some of which I'll discuss in later chapters. The information I've given you here should help you begin to pick out the features you'll need on your new driver. If you can find one that fits your swing tendencies, consider treating yourself to a new weapon.

"Give him the ball. He wants the ball!"

3

Why Golf Is the Greatest Game

David Grimes

Golf was invented by Scots, the same people who invented bagpipes, haggis, and skirts for men. In this context, golf makes perfect sense.

In 1457, King James II of Scotland declared the game illegal because it was taking time away from his army's archery practice. Golf, then, could be considered one of the first instruments for world peace.

In 1567, Mary, queen of Scots, was criticized for playing golf a few days after the murder of her husband, Lord Darnley. Golf, therefore, was on the cutting edge of the women's liberation movement, though "cutting edge" is probably not a good choice of words when talking about Mary, queen of Scots.

The first golf balls were leather covers stuffed with chicken feathers. This is how the word "McNugget" originated.

After a frustrating day on the links, golfers down through the

ages have mused that golf is "flog" spelled backwards. No one has ever sat at a bar after a hard day of running, biking, and swimming and mused that "nolhtairt" is triathlon spelled backwards.

No one plays golf for exercise. Do not gamble with a man who tells you otherwise because he is not to be trusted. One of the great golfers of the 1940s was a man named Porky Oliver. A few years ago, *Golf Digest* started a campaign to get golfers to walk instead of driving around in electric carts. The campaign generated a lot of laughs, much like one of Pat Paulsen's presidential campaigns. Speaking of laughs, one of the better golfers of the 1930s was a man by the name of Ky Laffoon.

Just because golf is not played for exercise does not mean you cannot injure yourself while doing it, thereby giving yourself a story with which you can bore people at cocktail parties. Last year, I threw my back out by bending over to pick up my nine iron. I am feeling much better now, thank you.

Thanks, in part, to Tiger Woods, golf has suddenly become "cool." I am not at all sure that this is a good thing, but it happened, so I guess I have to deal with it. Bill Murray plays golf. Kevin Costner plays golf. Hootie and the Blowfish play golf. Dan Quayle and Bill Clinton play golf. Like I said, I'm not at all convinced that this is a good thing.

Golf courses tend to wind through and around woods and lakes, which means you're likely to see lots of critters. On public courses in Manatee and Sarasota counties, I've seen bobcat, deer, wild turkey, otters, eagles, ospreys, scrub jays, alligators and, once, a rattlesnake that was about eight feet long and as big around in the middle as my thigh. Which is another good thing about golf carts—you can escape nature quickly if you need to.

The rules of golf are ridiculously complex, which is the way the rules of a superior game should be. When golfers are not betting or swearing, chances are they're arguing about the rules. Nobody, with the possible exception of Frank Hannigan, understands the rules of golf, least of all the touring pros. Paul Azinger was disqualified from a big tournament in Miami in 1991 because he violated rule 13–4 and failed to add the two-stroke penalty before signing his scorecard. A TV viewer caught the infraction and busted Azinger who, needless to say, was not pleased. Roberto de Vicenzo lost a Masters once because he incorrectly signed for a score higher than what he actually shot. "I am such a stupid," poor Roberto lamented when he realized what he had done. De Vicenzo may have lost the Masters, but he inadvertently uttered one of the greatest golf lines of all time, right up there with "it's still your turn" and "you might want to hit a provisional."

There are many other reasons why golf is the greatest game, but if I say any more it will encourage you to play and I certainly wouldn't want to do that as the courses are crowded enough already.

4

Mr. Hogan

Frank Fenton

I n the mid- to late 1980s I was research and development manager in charge of golf club design at the Ben Hogan Company when it was still at its original location on West Pafford Street in Fort Worth, Texas. This was the very same spot where Mr. Hogan had started his club company in 1953, on the site of a former gas station and plumbing shop. That was the same year he won the Masters, U.S. Open, and British Open. Not a bad year for Mr. Hogan.

You'll note that I refer to Ben Hogan as "Mr. Hogan." This is a sign of respect that all of us who worked with Mr. Hogan gave to him. It wasn't required. We all just did it. Even though Mr. Hogan had long ago sold the company to the AMF Corporation (and then later, several other concerns acquired the Ben Hogan Company), we all thought of him as the boss. Of course, there were AMF corporate people and Hogan Company officers to please, but we all knew that Mr. Hogan had to approve of a product before we released it to the public. If he didn't like or approve of a particular product, you could be sure that he would not sugar coat his feelings.

The sales force for the Hogan Company was made up of many very good players, and Mr. Hogan's approval was paramount to their support of the product. If he thought it was no good, the salesmen didn't try very hard to sell it. "What would Mr. Hogan think of this?" The thought was always in the back of our minds as we worked on new product and golf club ideas. It always made us research our ideas a little more in depth. Even if the product was something to help high-handicap golfers and a golfer like Mr. Hogan was not the intended user, we did our research in such a way that he would understand and appreciate the benefits of the club. If we could show valid reasons why something worked for a golfer, then he was on our side.

One reason this relationship with Mr. Hogan was so important was because, at that time, most of the Hogan golf clubs sold were sold through golf pro shops located at what are called "green grass" golf courses. A select group of club pros were designated as Home Staff Professionals for the Hogan Company. Each year an even smaller group of the Home Staff Professionals were invited to visit the plant in Fort Worth, play golf at Shady Oaks (Mr. Hogan's club), and attend a cocktail party and dinner with Mr. Hogan and other members of the company.

At one of the first dinners I attended during my time there, I saw hardened, grown men weep at the opportunity to sit and talk with Mr. Hogan. At first I didn't know what to think of it. Being younger members of the staff at that time, some of my contemporaries and I thought that perhaps the cocktails and wine had caused it. Mr. Hogan's playing days were over long before I ever met him, and at my age I didn't understand these more senior pros' feelings. But as the years went on and I began to learn many of the details of Mr. Hogan's career, I began to understand their feelings toward him. Never underestimate the power of a true legend in the eyes of the people who support your company. We had one at the Ben Hogan Company.

5

Japan and Taiwan

Frank Fenton

One of the beautiful things about the game of golf and the golf business is that you can play and work around the world, sometimes with people who do not even speak your language, and still have a great time. During my business travels overseas, I occasionally would have the opportunity to play golf with my hosts.

On one trip to Japan and Taiwan, I remember first getting business out of the way at a foundry on the outskirts of Kaohsiung in Taiwan. Kaohsiung is a crowded industrial area where many of the world's name-brand goods are made and shipped. Foundries everywhere in the world are usually hot, dirty environments, but this is especially true in Kaohsiung. I was there to oversee the making of the masters and molds for some clubs I had designed. This meant attending a meeting with the people who worked at the foundry. Often there would be a group of people in these meetings which included the head of the foundry, the English-speaking interpreter, the note-taking secretary, the engineers, and various other aides. At this particular meeting, I was getting nowhere with explaining the details of the design and specifications of the club heads through the interpreter to the head of the foundry, then on to the engineers. There were just too many people in the chain of the conversation. Finally I began to draw the club head shapes on a blackboard and use standard club-making terms like loft, roll and bulge, lie angle, and face angle. The engineers immediately understood what I was doing since they were familiar with these terms from the spec sheets they had previously seen. We sat and communicated this way for the remainder of the meeting. Even though I didn't speak Chinese and the engineers didn't speak English, we were speaking "golf" with each other. The masters and molds were made without further problems.

On this same trip, we continued on to Japan to meet with the people who ran the division of Spalding Sports Worldwide in that country. We did most of our work in Tokyo and enjoyed the hospitality of our hosts in this great city. After all the work was done we made plans to play golf at a course outside of Tokyo. I was told that it was not far, but like all travel in and around this congested area, it took over an hour to get to the golf course by car.

The course had two complete sets of greens on each hole. One green on each hole had perfect-looking grass, perhaps a type of bent grass. These greens were roped off and were only there for show. The actual greens that we played on were made up of bumpy, rough-looking zoysia grass. It was a real challenge trying to putt on these. But what the heck, we were there to take pleasure in the game and enjoy the companionship of our playing partners. Then it began to rain. The cotton sweater I had on began to grow down toward my knees. Each step made it elongate further. If I had been playing better I might have seen the humor in this, but the round, like my sweater, just seemed to get longer.

My caddie was an energetic young man who tried his best to help. Since he did not speak English and my Japanese is extremely limited, we communicated in the universal language of golf. Everywhere golf is played, a driver is a driver, a five iron is a five iron, and a putter is a putter—right? I thought so for a good part of the round, until I was faced with a shot on one hole that I estimated to be 215 yards or so to an uphill green. My caddie was on the opposite side of the fairway helping another player in our group, so I called over, "How far?" so that I could determine what club to ask for. He looked at me strangely, so I yelled a little louder, "How far?" This time he smiled and nodded and ran over to me with a four iron. I thought that I had grossly misjudged the distance, so I trusted his selection and solidly struck the number four. I was easily thirty yards short of the green. My faithful caddie looked at me with pity in his eyes, as if I had selected the four iron myself and had just failed to hit it home. I checked with my Japanese playing partner, who informed me that my caddie thought I'd said, "Now four," instructing him that I wanted to hit the number four iron.

We had a good laugh at this as the rain finally quit. The sun was coming out, and while we were waiting on the next tee, my playing partners told me another Japanese caddie story. You may have seen pictures of the women caddies in Japan who wear large hoods over their heads. These women are generally very good caddies, but many of them have never played golf. One time my Japanese friend was playing and asked his caddie how far it was to the crest of the hilltop in the fairway where he intended to hit his drive. The petite lady caddie pondered this for a moment and then peered out from under her large hood and said confidently, "Three or four minutes by walking." The language of golf is universal, and so are caddie stories.

When we finished the eighteenth hole I looked up to see the path to the clubhouse go up a slope to a hill that looked to rise fifteen stories above us. My tired legs would have a real job hauling me and my thirty-pound wet sweater up this hill. My congenial caddie pointed out a conveyor belt with a rubberized walkway on it that carried us up the hill like a bag of groceries. I was never so happy to see Japanese ingenuity at work.

6

Golf: Very Important

David Grimes

I n yet another moving episode in the dramatic series "Why Men Are Jerks," Japan's prime minister has come under fire for continuing with his game of golf after learning that a U.S. submarine had struck a Japanese fishing boat, killing nine.

Prime Minister Yoshiro Mori, who has seen his standing in the popularity polls drop to that of week-old sushi, defended his actions by saying it is unwise to get "flustered" in a crisis.

"It would not get any of us anywhere if I rushed to (the prime minister's official residence) and got all flustered without receiving reports," Mori told reporters. "We took the safest course of action."

Mori's action, or lack of it, is pretty typical of avid golfers I know. Give them the choice between golf and world peace and most would answer, "Nine holes or eighteen?"

In that context, it should come as no surprise that Mori

would prefer the challenge of a three-foot downhill putt with a slight left-to-right break to dealing with a messy international incident.

It reminded me of the time I was playing golf with my attorney, Jaws, and an employee from the clubhouse came barreling up to us in a golf cart.

"Sir, we just got a call from your wife!" the employee told Jaws breathlessly. "She's hemorrhaging and wants you to come home right away!"

"Right now?" Jaws replied incredulously. "But I'm three under par with only four to play!"

The fact that Jaws and his wife divorced shortly after that is not the point of the story. The point, from the perspective of an avid golfer who is having the round of his life, is how one interprets the word "hemorrhage." Are we talking about a cut finger or a severed limb? Is there blood on the floor? How much? A teaspoon? A cup? A quart? Is there something in the house—a tie, perhaps, or maybe a belt—with which she could tie off the gushing artery until her husband finishes playing eighteen, a downhill, downwind par-five that he could easily reach in two, leading to a birdie or possibly even an eagle? How can she be thinking of herself at a time like this?

Before you women accuse me of being crass and insensitive, allow me to point out that I am not suggesting that Prime Minister Mori was having the round of his life the morning the trawler was hit by the sub. The press, which always seems to overlook the important details, failed to mention how Mori was playing that particular day, focusing instead on the wreck, the loss of life, and a bunch of other stuff that had nothing to do with the speed of the greens or how the prime minister was managing his slice and his deep-seated fear of long-iron shots over water.

My guess is that the prime minister did not have a particularly good day on the links due to his aides constantly bothering him with updates on the collision and the constant ring of cell phones. (Another good reason not to allow cell phones on the golf course, by the way.) He may even have gotten "flustered," the very thing he was trying so hard to avoid. And that will drive your score up quicker than anything.

7

Cost of Clubs

Frank Fenton

Since I live in Florida, I run into quite a few older golfers who have been playing the game for many years and remember when clubs cost a lot less money than they do today. I'd venture to say that these same folks remember when a nice home cost $25,000 and a fine automobile was only $2,000. Of course people made much less money at their jobs back then, too.

I try to explain that golf clubs, like almost everything else, cost more today due to inflation, labor, marketing costs, and the higher costs of components (club heads, shafts, grips, etc.). The suppliers of components are under the same pressures of inflation, labor, etc., as the golf club manufacturers.

One of the real reasons that modern clubs cost so much more than they did thirty to forty years ago is that many of the more expensive pro-line golf clubs are made with very costly high-tech materials. Most drivers today are sold with high-end graphite shafts rather than steel. These high-tech composite shafts are beneficial to golfers and are worth the money, so this is what golf companies sell. A properly fitted graphite shaft can do so much to help a golfer's game that almost all golfers are willing to pay the extra price. The thing is—especially on a driver—that the equipment made with costlier materials is no longer seen as an extra but as a necessary feature. Sort of like air conditioning in a car. Not too many cars are sold without AC these days (at least not down here in Florida), but I remember as a kid always having to crank down the window to get cool air. Most younger kids now think cars with roll-down window handles are quaint—I know my kids do. Just as air conditioning, power windows, and automatic transmissions have become necessary features on an automobile, so too have graphite shafts and titanium club heads become necessary items for the golfer today.

Not too many years ago, the finest drivers and fairway woods were actually made of wood. Some were laminated hard rock maple, but the premium ones were made from oil-hardened persimmon. Metal woods, with their hollow-shell bodies and extreme perimeter weighting, created woods that were easier to hit, more forgiving (due to their higher moment of inertia, which aids the club head's resistance to twisting on off-center hits), and more durable than the real wooden club heads. When designers began to explore further improvements of metal woods they found that even larger sizes with strong walls could be made from titanium (Ti). Ti metal woods were initially thought to be too costly to sell to the general public, but the benefits were there and golfers proved they were willing to pay the extra price.

Golf club designers found ways to incorporate Ti into some clubs by using it only in the face area to take advantage of its high strength-to-weight ratio. By removing steel faces and replacing them with the lighter Ti, the perimeter weighting was enhanced (once again increasing the moment of inertia of the club head). This was done on some wood-type clubs by casting the main body from steel or aerospace-grade aluminum and then using the Ti face. Some sets of irons were made with this same technique, but the main body of the iron club head would generally be steel.

On top of all these high-tech, pricey materials, some club heads actually began to have additional elements attached to them. Tungsten, a very heavy metal, is strategically placed in the club head to add extra weighting to the perimeter (as designers are always trying to create a higher moment of inertia). Brass, copper, copper tungsten, and the old reliable lead are used in this same manner.

Any time that you begin to use exotic materials or attach extra items like face inserts, perimeter weights, and so forth, you add cost and labor to the price of the club head. Add in the marketing cost to get the manufacturers' message out to the public and to have big-name Tour players use the manufacturers' clubs, and you have what you might believe to be a high-priced golf club.

Golf club prices may not seem as high as you thought after you consider all these items I have mentioned. If your golf clubs fit you properly and you cherish playing the game with them, then the price is all relative. Look for a set that fits your needs and enjoy.

8

Center of Gravity

Frank Fenton

I would like to take some time to explain a phrase that you hear more and more each month from golf club manufacturers. The term "center of gravity" or "CG" is used very often these days in reference to golf clubs. Sometimes the more vague term "sweet spot" is used to help market these clubs. Though the technical definition of CG is more complex, all you need to know to improve your game is that an object's CG is the object's single finite balance point in all directions. Club heads can have a low CG, high CG, a CG located close to the face, or one located deeper in toward the rear of the head.

For example, take a metal wood head off its golf shaft and then find the point where you can balance this head on the tip of a pin with the face of the club pointing down, parallel to a table top. Mark this balance spot on the face. Now balance the same head in its normal playing position, with the sole of the club head parallel to the table top. Again, mark this spot. Do the same balancing trick (if you can) on the curved areas of the crown (top) of the club head and the rear of the club head. If you can, also do the balancing test on the toe and heel areas of the club head. Now you have mapped out many of the balance points of the club head. If you can then imagine that this head is made of clear glass and that you can see all these balance points converging into one finite point inside the club head, you would be visualizing the club head's CG. The exact point may also be calculated by club designers by using a computer and feeding in all the known specifications of the club head's outside dimensions, wall thickness, and various materials, as well as any heavy screw, back weight, or weight chip locations that would affect the CG.

The two converging CG locations that you will be most interested in are the face spot and sole spot that you marked. The face spot tells you how high up, from the lower leading edge of the club face, the CG is located. If this spot is closer to the lower edge than to the top edge of the club face, the club head is said to be a low-CG club head. With a low-CG club head, you can get the ball up in the air quicker and easier by having the club face CG spot contact the ball below its own CG spot (which is located inside the center of the ball at the equator). Most golfers want this effect and would probably prefer a low-CG club head. Stronger-hitting golfers who want to keep the ball flight down and get a lower trajectory shot with more roll would prefer a club head with a higher CG.

The balance spot you marked on the sole will also tell you how the head will affect ball flight. If the CG spot on the sole is located close to the face edge on the sole, the club head will tend to present itself to the ball at impact with close to the actual measured loft of the club head at address (although almost all golfers have the golf shaft bowed slightly forward at impact, thus creating some additional loft). If the CG spot on the club head's sole is located farther back in, toward the rear of the head (which is often accomplished by adding a back weight to the rear of the head), then this CG location will cause the rear of the club head to be pulled downward as it travels toward the ball just before impact, bowing the shaft forward even more than normal, creating an increased amount of loft to be presented to the ball, and causing the ball to fly off with a higher trajectory (this is known as "dynamic loft"). A golfer looking to get the ball up in the air would appreciate a golf club head with its sole's CG spot toward the rear of head.

All this may sound complicated but it is just like television—you don't have to understand all the details of how television signals work to enjoy watching it. With golf clubs, all you need to know is that a low-CG club head will help get the ball up in the air for you more easily than a club head with a high CG. If you need help hitting the ball on a higher trajectory, try out one of the many clubs that have a low CG.

9

Grimes' Laws of Golf

David Grimes

Non-golfers may be familiar with Murphy's Law, which states that everything that can go wrong *will* go wrong. Golfers are more likely to view Murphy as an optimist. Florida golf, in particular, is so perverse and disheartening that Murphy's disciples long ago abandoned the game in favor of more relaxing pastimes such as fire-walking and sword-swallowing. The hardy souls who have remained behind to battle the alligator-infested bogs, rattlesnake-filled woods and double-breaking greens have come up with their own set of laws, corollaries, axioms, precepts, revelations, and criteria intended to explain the inexplicable things that happen on the golf course. A knowledge of these laments will do nothing to lower your score, but you may derive comfort in knowing that much of the suffering you endure out there is out of your control.

Murphy's Law of Advance Tee Times

If you make your tee time three days in advance, the next two days are sure to be gloriously sunny and warm, with little wind. On the third day, however, a cold front will blow down from northern Saskatchewan, sending temperatures plummeting into a frosty zone that one normally associates with ice fishing rather than golf. Your "I Love Florida" T-shirt will offer scant protection from the freezing wind, which will always be in your face on long par fours and bunker shots, helping to scour off those facial imperfections your dermatologist missed.

Dante's Law of Reward and Punishment (Mostly Punishment)

Nature will always reveal your flaws. If you are cursed with a slice, the wind will blow from left to right on every shot you hit. Playing in the opposite direction will not help; the wind will shift. If you are unskilled at bunker shots, you will see more sand than Moammar Khadafy. If you tend to misjudge long putts, your ball will never finish closer than sixty feet from the hole. If iron shots over water make you nervous, you will send a small bucket to a watery grave. The best shot you strike all day will hit a sprinkler head and bounce out of bounds.

Dave's Rule of Surlyn Conservation

The cheaper the ball, the harder it is to lose. Conversely, the new, high-tech sleeve of balls that you bought in the pro shop for $15 will leap out of your bag on the way to the first tee and drown itself in a tar pit.

"I told you not to use him as a caddy!"

Wheezer's First Law of Fallibility

No good shot will go unpunished. Your best drive of the day will be immediately followed by an ugly shank into the quicksand. The brilliant lob-wedge shot that you feathered over the bunker to within inches of the pin will be followed, at the next opportunity, by a wretched chunk that travels all of two feet or a screaming fizzer that nearly kneecaps your partner on the other side of the green. A birdie pretty much guarantees that your score on the next hole will be an "X."

Redfish's Law of Thermodynamics

Things get worse under pressure. The more important the match or tournament, the worse you will play. An eight-handicapper will suddenly find himself unable to break ninety. A fourteen-handicapper will be challenged to stay on the south side of one hundred. Normally straight drivers will, by the end of the day, be teeing off with a seven iron just to keep the ball in play. The next day, after the tournament is over, you will shoot the lowest round of your life.

Sideshow Bob's Pontification Postulate

The higher the handicap of the golfer, the more qualified he will deem himself to offer instruction. These fonts of knowledge can recite from memory every golfing platitude uttered since Og told Magog to keep her eye on the ball. Favorites include "You came over the top," "Fire the left side," and the always popular "Don't overswing."

Mulligan's Rule of Threes

New golf balls from the same sleeve tend to follow one another into water hazards, into the tops of palm trees, or out of bounds. (See Dave's Rule of Surlyn Conservation.) It is best to get rid of all three of your new balls on the first hole so you can enjoy the rest of your round.

Foozle's Retribution Precept

Any disparaging remark you make about a partner's or opponent's shot—no matter how light-hearted its intent—will result in your immediately hitting a shot that is far worse. The

Retribution Precept cannot be fooled by sarcasm, by the way. If you say "nice try" when your partner muffs a straight uphill two-footer, you will, at some point during the day, miss a putt even shorter.

Some days you win and some days you lose. But the game of golf will always have the last laugh.

10

Shafts: Cycles Per Minute

Frank Fenton

Over the next few chapters I will share some of my knowledge relating to the golf club shaft. Since this seemingly simple object has so many features and specifications that are important to its function, I will spread out this explanation over several chapters. In this chapter I'll explain shaft frequency or cycles per minute (CPM).

The purpose of determining a shaft's frequency is to ascertain its overall stiffness. If a shaft vibrates at a high CPM reading, it is stiffer than one that moves at a slower vibration. As an example, try placing a foot-long ruler on the end of your desk. If you hold it down with two inches on the flat desktop surface and the rest of the ruler hanging off the edge of your desk and then pull down on the hanging end, you will see a slow vibration of the ruler tip. Next, move the ruler so that you are holding down five inches of the end clamped to the flat desktop. Pull the tip end down with the same force as before and you'll see a much-faster vibration on the tip end. In the second instance, the ruler is much stiffer than in the first.

Golf shafts, whether they are made of steel, graphite, titanium, or some other material, all have a certain CPM reading. This measurement is taken on a shaft frequency machine. There are numerous types of these machines made by multiple companies. In all cases, the butt end of the shaft (or sometimes the assembled club) is securely clamped. The rest of the shaft is pulled or plucked at the tip (or head) end so that it vibrates—usually in an up-and-down motion like the ruler in the example above. The shaft's CPM is then measured by how fast the vibrating tip end is moving up and down from its low point to its high point (this range is called the cycle). This movement may be measured by a photoelectric eye, or, in the case of steel shafts, by a magnetic device. Since magnets don't work with the non-metallic composite shafts, the eye is the more common method. As in the ruler example above, a shaft with a higher CPM reading is stiffer than one with a lower CPM reading. This may sound complicated, but it is a simple, quick task that tells golf club manufacturers the overall stiffness of a shaft.

What features of the shaft determine the CPM or frequency? There are many, but I'll discuss only the most important ones, which are design, material, weight, and finished length. The design of a shaft is one of the most important factors in determining the stiffness. With steel shafts, the relevant features are the position of the shaft steps (which are put on the shafts during the manufacturing process) and the shaft's outside diameter (OD). Generally, the larger the shaft OD and the lower this large OD is positioned toward the tip end of the shaft, the stiffer the shaft is (assuming wall thicknesses are standard).

In the case of composite or graphite shafts, which usually don't have steps, design and materials have to work together. Stiffness is built into the shaft by the use of different wall thicknesses, shaft ODs, composite material locations, and placement angles of materials during manufacturing. All this means that a light shaft could be stiffer than a heavy shaft. Don't get fooled into thinking that a heavy shaft is always stiffer than a lighter shaft.

Now, if two shafts are identical in design and material, they can still have different degrees of stiffness because of their weight. The best-known example of this is the steel Dynamic shaft versus the steel Dynamic Gold shaft. These are exactly the same shafts except that the standard Dynamic shaft has a wider weight tolerance of about ±3.5 grams (still pro-line specs, of course). Some of the shafts are sorted out to much tighter weight tolerances (less than ±1 gram), and these become the Dynamic Gold. Rather than have just one stiff flex (S-flex), the Dynamic Gold shafts have multiple S-flexes, from the lightest and softer-flex S100 through to the heavier and firmer S500. If you were to test these Dynamic Gold shafts (remember that they are exactly the same design) on a frequency machine in their various weights, you would find that the CPM readings get slightly higher each time the weight increases. Under these circumstances, more weight does mean the shaft is stiffer.

Finally, if you build a club to a longer or shorter finished length than another club with exactly the same shaft design, material, and weight, you will affect the CPM reading also. Remember the ruler example.

So, I have shown you several ways a golf shaft can have different CPMs—design, material, weight, and finished length. In the next few chapters I'll explain other shaft features such as kick point, torque, shaft weight, and balance point. All of these features may help your game if you know what to look for.

11

Shafts: Kick Point

Frank Fenton

In this chapter, I will explain a feature of golf shafts that is little understood but often bandied about by golfers. You may have heard one of your golfing companions praising his new driver. He might have said how much easier it was to get the ball up in the air due to the new club shaft's lower kick point. What in the world does that mean—lower kick point? Shouldn't that mean the ball goes lower? Wouldn't a higher kick point make the ball go higher? What the heck is a kick point? Follow along with me and I'll make this easy to understand.

After golf shaft manufacturers design a shaft with certain performance characteristics, they make a small run of proto-type shafts. They check to be sure that the proper kick point (sometimes referred to as the flex point) has been created from the design by performing a simple test. The shaft is horizontal-ly positioned in a device that clamps or holds the butt end (the large-diameter end that the grip will be over) in place, and a standard amount of weight or some downward pressure from a machine is exerted on the tip end (the smaller-diameter end that the golf head will be assembled to). The butt-end portion of the horizontally-fixed shaft will remain horizontal, but as the pressure of the weight is felt on the shaft tip, a curve appears as the lower section of the shaft tip begins to droop downward. The point at which the downward curve appears is known as the kick point. Using a standard to grade this new shaft's kick point against, golf shaft designers can ascertain if the new shaft has a low, mid, or high kick point. What should be understood, however, is that there is very little actual, physical difference in the location of a low kick point versus that of a high kick point on a shaft. The locations of these different kick points probably fall within a couple of inches from each other. In all cases the kick point is positioned approximately just below the halfway point of the shaft length, toward the tip.

This is not to say that the kick point location makes no difference in the playing performance of a shaft. The kick point of a shaft will determine the initial launch trajectory of the ball flight (along with club head loft and center of gravity). Having the kick point positioned in a higher spot will make the lower part of the shaft feel firmer and the shaft flex ever-so-slightly higher up the shaft, causing the ball to be launched on a somewhat lower trajectory. The ball flight from the shaft with a lower kick point will be initially slightly higher (which makes it easier for many golfers to get the ball in the air) due to the butt end of the shaft feeling slightly stiffer and the tip end having more flexibility. There are many players on the men's PGA Tour that use higher-flex-point shafts to keep the ball from ballooning on their tee shots. They feel that this gives them more control of their ball flight and allows them to keep the ball out of the wind as well as to get more roll for added distance. This in turn leads to their hitting more fairways and winning more money. Many players on the LPGA Tour use shafts that have lower flex points to aid in getting the ball flight up. These women like not only the ease with which the ball is launched into the air, but also the slightly softer feel of this type of shaft. As I have said previously, most average male golfers would be better off emulating the LPGA player's shaft choice, since their club head speeds are closer to the lady pros' rather than the men's.

Now that you understand what a kick point is, you should take a look at your ball flight difficulties and see if a shaft with a higher or lower kick point would be beneficial to your game. If you need to hit the ball higher, you should try a shaft with a lower kick point. Conversely, if you want to hit the ball lower, you should try a shaft that has its kick point higher toward the butt end of the shaft. This is yet another golf shaft characteristic that, when fit properly to your swing, can help make you a better golfer.

12

Getting the Knack of the Golf Cliché

David Grimes

Forget swing thoughts and high-tech equipment; the thing that separates a good golfer from a bad golfer is his or her knowledge of clichés. If you're just taking up the game, you'll want to stick with the most basic of clichés, taking care to utter them in the proper situation. "That won't hurt you" and its corollary, "That dog will hunt," are examples of basic golf clichés. They're usually said when a golfer hits an exceptional shot, but they're also appropriate when a golfer hits an indifferent shot that "works out." Some people utter this cliché when a golfer hits a terrible shot that will surely result in a triple bogey, but that kind of irony is best left to the professionals or those adept at ducking thrown clubs.

A putt that is left short gives you many opportunities to show off your knowledge of golf clichés. The most common are "Nice putt, Alice" or "Does your husband play?" These work less well if the person you are addressing is a woman named Alice.

It's unclear how a putt left short and sexism became intertwined, but that's the way it is, and the golfer who wishes to show off his facility with clichés has no choice but to go with the flow. Variants on "Nice putt, Alice" include "I got my putter stuck in my bra" and the similarly lingerie-themed, "Wearing your wife's undies today?"

Since bad shots far outnumber good shots in golf, it is no surprise that most clichés refer to a shot that turns out less than perfectly. "I see you're driving with your pitching wood today" is a reference to a high, short-tee shot, as are "Houston, we have a problem," "rainmaker," "Fore, Lord!" and "Nice punt."

Military themes recur in golf clichés, possibly because the game so often seems like war and you're on the losing side. "Army golf" refers to shots that miss the mark on both sides (left, right, left, right). A "Rommel" is a shot that travels from one sand trap to another, and a "Hitler" means you failed to get out of the bunker. If your playing partners dub you "Lawrence of Arabia," that means you've spent an inordinate amount of time that day in the sand traps.

"Incoming" is a warning to your fellow players to pay attention as your shot may go anywhere, and "depth charge" refers to a long putt that goes in.

If you "nuke it," you haven't started World War III; you've simply hit a long drive. The term is also used disparagingly to describe a putt struck way too hard. There are almost as many clichés for putts of this sort as there are for putts left short, which should give you a clue that there are lots of bad putters out there. Other clichés for overzealous putts include "grow hair," "hit a house," "hit a wall," "hit something," "deploy chute"

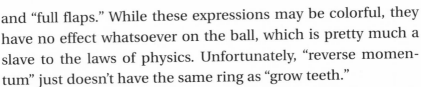

and "full flaps." While these expressions may be colorful, they have no effect whatsoever on the ball, which is pretty much a slave to the laws of physics. Unfortunately, "reverse momentum" just doesn't have the same ring as "grow teeth."

The laws of physics seldom work in the golfer's favor, which explains the term "cellophane bridge," used to describe a putt that seemingly rolls over the hole without falling in. Other clichés include "mother-in-law putt" (nothing but lip) and an "Argentina" (one revolution shy of going in).

Golfers quickly learn that the most satisfying shot in golf is the "gimmee," a short putt that your opponent concedes and doesn't make you hole out. While it's considered unseemly to beg for gimmees, that doesn't mean golfers don't do it. It is fine sport indeed to torture those poor souls for whom a three-foot putt is a torment worthy of Dante's *Inferno*. Golfers let the pathetic, whimpering slob know that the putt is not a gimmee by saying things like "there's some chicken left on that bone," "there's some foam left on that beer," or—as some said during the final days of his term—"there's some Clinton left in that administration."

This is just a sampling of the hundreds of golf clichés out there. The longer you play, the more clichés you'll learn, until finally you realize that your conversation consists of nothing but golf clichés. When that day comes, you'll know you're a real golfer.

13

Shafts: Torque

Frank Fenton

Since I believe that the golf shaft is the engine that runs the club, I have explained some of the different aspects of golf shafts. In this chapter I will explain what a golf shaft's torque is. I have always thought that the name for this specification should be the "torque reading," since we must apply torque to the shaft to generate this particular reading; but since torque is the commonly-used term, I shall stick with it here.

First let me explain what torque is when discussing golf shafts. If you were to hold your driver grip very securely in one hand and then firmly twist the club head face open with your other hand, you would see or feel a small amount of rotation from the club head end, even though the grip end would not be moving. To illustrate with another simple example, get a drink and two straws. Use one straw for your drink and the other one for this demonstration. Hold one end of the straw firmly in the fingertips of your left hand. Grab the other end of the straw with the fingertips of your right hand. Do not move your left fingers, and using only your right fingers, twist the straw along its length. You are applying torque to the straw. Notice how the walls of the straw rotate along its length. You are seeing what a tube will do under a torque load. A golf shaft is mainly a tube, albeit a strong, resilient, expensive one.

When golf shaft manufacturers check the torque reading of a shaft in the factory (which is measured in units called "foot pounds"), the shaft is not yet assembled into a finished club. They securely clamp the butt end of the shaft in a fixture that keeps it from moving. Then they clamp the tip end in another fixture so that it may be "torqued" or rotated about the center-line of the shaft's linear axis. The fixtures used may be as simple as a lever with a weight hanging on it or as high-tech as an elec-tronic device that exerts one foot pound of torque to the end of the shaft. The measurement "one foot pound" refers to the fact that, originally, technicians would clamp a one-foot-long lever to the tip end of the shaft while a one-pound weight was hung from the far end of the lever. Some companies test their shafts to a higher foot pound load, but the industry generally uses one foot pound of torque when comparing shafts.

What is read are the degrees of twist the shaft rotates about its linear axis under this force. Readings of three or four degrees are common. If a shaft is tested and found to twist three degrees under a one-foot-pound load, it is said to have three degrees of torque and to have less torque than a shaft that twists six degrees under the same load. A shaft with a high torque is one that twists more compared to a shaft with a low torque.

Now that you understand what torque is and how it is measured, why should you care? Because the torque in a shaft will at least partially determine how you hit the golf ball. A shaft with a lot of torque, when swung by a strong, skilled golfer, will not be as accurate as a shaft with less torque. Due to the twisting of the shaft during the golf swing, the club face may be presented back to the ball too early or too late, causing shots to vary in their line of flight. A shaft with too much torque may also feel like it is too "tip weak" for this stronger golfer, since it may launch the ball on a higher trajectory.

One would think, then, that it makes sense to have a golf shaft with zero degrees of torque. But this is not the case. As shaft designers developed shafts with lower and lower torques, it was discovered that having too low of a torque will make the shaft feel hard and harsh and much too stiff on the tip end. A few years back, with the help of some other engineers, I patented one of the first oversize-tip composite graphite shafts that are now so popular with golf companies. The idea was that if we could increase the outside diameter (OD) of the shaft tip, we could reduce the undesirable torque that was prevalent on all but the most expensive-material graphite shafts of that period. This method worked really well to reduce the torque—so well, in fact, that the prototype shafts felt too stiff and harsh and made it difficult to launch a ball on a playable trajectory. We were finally able to overcome this problem by making the overall shaft flex softer and bringing the torques to a usable level.

Average steel shafts have about two degrees of torque when on an iron shaft and around two and a half degrees on a wood shaft. Interestingly enough, these seem to be the numbers that most good golfers settle on for their modern-day graphite shafts. Out on the PGA Tour, players seem to prefer two to three degrees of torque on their drivers. Players on the LPGA Tour (who have swing speeds more similar to those of average male amateur golfers) seem to like shafts with three and a half to four and a half degrees of torque. Clearly, some amount of torque helps make the club feel proper and aids in the timing for the golfer. Since LPGA players generally swing slower than the male Tour players, they are less concerned with a minor degree of shaft twist and more interested in the launch and feel that the shaft generates. To the male Tour player, being off-line at 280 yards from the tee is a much greater problem than for the LPGA player at 240 yards out.

What sort of things in a shaft will affect its torque reading? As I stated, most steel shafts tend to have similar torques of about two to two and a half degrees. Graphite composite shafts, however, can be designed and produced with all different types of torques. The type of material, the angle and location in which those materials are put into the shaft, the wall thickness, and the shaft's outside diameter are some of the factors that will affect a composite shaft's torque. As far as drivers go, if you need help getting the ball up in the air, shafts that have a lower kick point (one that is closer to the club head) will launch the ball on a higher trajectory; these types of shafts often have a higher torque. If you need to feel the club head more as you bring it down to impact the ball, or you are hanging the ball off to the right, a shaft with more torque may also be for you. Try out something in the four- to five-degree range. If, on the other hand, you strive for accuracy and already swing at a pretty fast speed, I would recommend that you try a shaft with lower torque, somewhere around two and a half to three and a half degrees. Don't go below two degrees with your driver unless you have a very high swing speed.

I hope that this information on the golf shaft's torque reading will help you select a shaft that best fits your swing.

14

Shafts: Weight, Balance Point, and Swing Weight

Frank Fenton

This chapter will explain the purpose of the shaft's balance point and its overall weight in relation to the finished club's swing weight.

The balance point of a golf shaft is the actual center of gravity (CG) of the shaft when it is balanced on a sharp edge in the horizontal position before it is installed in the club. The balance point measurement is the distance from the tip end of the shaft up to the actual balance point. Let's say that you have a knife's edge facing skyward. If you were to balance a golf shaft on this edge and found that it balanced twenty-two inches from the tip end, you could compare this shaft with one that balanced, let's say, twenty-four inches from the tip end. In this example, the shaft with the twenty-two-inch balance point would make the assembled club read heavier on the swing weight scale.

Let me give you a brief explanation of what "swing weight" means and how it is measured. Golf club designers and manufacturers build finished clubs (including the grip, shaft, and club head) to a certain length, weight, and balance to create the "heft" of the club in your hands. This heft is measured on a swing weight scale, which is generally a type of fulcrum (like a see-saw). The butt end of the club (and a good part of the shaft and grip) is on one side of the fulcrum. The remainder of the shaft and the club head are on the other side of the fulcrum. There are a series of letter-number denominations known as "swing weight points" that start at the very light-feeling low end with A0 through A9 to B0, B1, and so on through the more common denominations of D0, D1, D2, etc. The very heavy swing weights would read in the E range on the swing weight scale, with the scale usually topping out at around the F or G range. The feel of the weight of the club hanging down from your hands and arms as you waggle the club is what the scale is trying to measure.

Let's suppose that the shafts in the example above have exactly the same weight shaft, head, grip, and overall weight. Even then, the shaft with the twenty-two-inch balance point may weigh D4 on the swing weight scale while the shaft with the twenty-four-inch balance point may weigh only D2, simply due to the first shaft's lower balance point. Part of the shaft weight is part of the swing weight. If the balance point of one type of golf shaft is closer to the head end than another type of shaft, then it will cause the swing weight scale to measure a higher (heavier) swing weight. This is not necessarily bad, it is just another factor the club builder must take into consideration when setting the specs for the finished club. As a matter of fact, sometimes club manufacturers achieve desired swing weights by tinkering with this. If a club manufacturer created club head tooling that produced heads to a specified weight to fit heavier steel shafts, he may also wish to pair up the heavy club heads with graphite (or lightweight steel) shafts with a lower balance point to get a more playable or marketable swing weight. Since the lower (and lighter) part of the lightweight shaft is part of the swing weight, you would normally have to create heavier heads to yield the same swing weight (at the same finished length, which is why so many graphite shafted clubs are normally made longer). This is really not as complicated as it all sounds. It is just a very precise balancing act by the club maker.

Now that you understand the factors that affect the swing weight of a club, let's talk about the purpose and benefits of a lighter- versus a heavier-weight shaft. Lighter-weight shafts allow club-makers to make the heads heavier and keep all the other specs (including the swing weight) the same. If the shafts are very light, the overall weight of the club may in fact go down. From a physics standpoint, this is all good. If I can hand you a finished golf club that has more mass on the business end of the club (the club head, which hits the ball) then you have a more efficient tool. This is especially true if you happen to hit the ball off the club head's CG. A club head that is heavier will have a higher moment of inertia and therefore will be more resistant to twisting about its CG and less likely to cause misdirected shots. A lighter-weight shaft may also help create an overall lighter club. This lighter club would be easier to swing faster or swing with more control than a heavier-weight club.

A favorite way for some club manufacturers to make lighter clubs is to use a lightweight shaft and remove some weight from the head so that a club with a much longer finished length can be produced with a conventional swing weight of D2 or D3. The club is lighter and longer overall, which can help produce greater distance shots. But I like to keep the mass in the club head, since this is what I hit the ball with. If the swing weight goes up some, say to D6, so be it. I am not too concerned with it, since this is what usually is done out on the PGA Tour when players' clubs are built. The PGA Senior Tour players, especially, seem to prefer a longer club with a heavier swing weight.

Another reason the Senior players like the lighter shafts is that they are usually softer in stiffness and have a lower kick point. However, light shafts can be made very stiff, too, with a stiffer tip section to make the kick point higher up the shaft (shaft tips with larger outside diameters are used to accomplish this as well as to lower the torque reading on a lightweight shaft). A lighter shaft (usually composite graphite) will also help absorb some of the undesirable shock from a golf shot, making it easier for the older players to practice and play longer. This shock-absorbing feature can also be obtained with a steel shaft such as the Sensicore that has a very narrow, lightweight plastic tube wrapped in foam inside the shaft.

Many of the players on the regular PGA Tour prefer a heavier shaft. This is because they believe the heavier shaft gives them the "feel" and balance of the overall club weight they are looking for and they don't mind swinging the extra weight. If you are as strong a swinger as some of these guys, a heavier club may actually help smooth out your swing and help maintain a better tempo. These players already have the strength to produce distance, but the name of the game on Tour is to hit what you aim at and make birdies. Because these younger players swing so hard, they also are looking for shafts that have lower torque. Low torque shafts are usually the heavier ones.

If you already have great club head speed and are looking for a smoother tempo, try a heavier shaft. But if you are like most golfers, you will need the advantage of a lightweight shaft (perhaps at a longer length for more distance). This lighter-weight shaft will give you an overall lighter club that should be easier to swing with more control and accuracy.

15

It Is Time to Ban Golfers Who Walk the Course

David Grimes

I agree with the Supreme Court ruling that allows disabled pro golfer Casey Martin to ride in a cart, but I wish the court had taken the matter a step further and banned walking altogether. Almost all golfers, with the exception of tour pros, ride around the course in a battery-powered golf cart, which is the way God and Jackie Gleason intended the game to be played. The few remaining fitness freaks who insist on walking are a major source of irritation to the rest of us who, thanks to on-course beers and ham-and-cheese sandwiches, actually manage to gain weight while playing.

Riding a golf cart has many advantages over walking. For one thing, a cart can get you back to the clubhouse faster for more beer or emergency administration of the Heimlich maneuver in case you choke on your ham-and-cheese sandwich. Carts also help golfers avoid painful leg cramps and the general muscle soreness that comes from walking long dis-

tances over hilly terrain. Walking can lead to dehydration, per-
spiration, and circulation, all things that tend to distract a
golfer's attention from the arrival of the beverage cart.

Some people thought that electric golf carts would speed up
the pace of play, but thankfully, that has not proven to be the
case. Golfers who ride in a cart take as long, if not longer, to finish their round as golfers who walk. This is because there are
two golfers to every golf cart and the Gods of Golf arrange it so
that their balls never wind up in the same county, let alone the
same fairway. As a result, much of cart-golf is spent traveling
side-to-side, like a crab, rather than forward. This eats up a lot
of time and pretty much guarantees that there will be insuffi-
cient daylight for any yard work once the golfer returns home.

Golfers like Jack Nicklaus who think riding removes the
stamina factor from golf underestimate the physical demands
of proper cart operation. For starters, very few carts are
equipped with power steering, meaning that the driver often
has to use two or more fingers to turn the wheel. Also, there are
times when you need to back up the cart, a maneuver that
requires you to bend over in a physically challenging way and
move a lever with what may or may not be your dominant hand.
Then—and this is where it gets especially grueling—to go forward again, you have to bend over again and shove the lever in
the opposite direction! Golfers who have to back up the cart
more than once usually quit after nine holes out of sheer
exhaustion.

Nicklaus also conveniently neglects to mention the three little words that drain the joy out of a rider's round before it
begins: Cart paths only. If the course is muddy, carts are not
permitted to leave the paved cart paths, meaning that golfers

sometimes have to walk thirty, forty, or, unbelievably, fifty yards to their ball, usually while carrying two or three clubs. This is an unspeakable hardship and could explain why so many golfers have moved to Florida, where it never rains. The Supreme Court is to be congratulated for making the right decision in the Casey Martin case. Maybe next time they'll get a chance to finish the job and make cart-riding mandatory for everyone.

16

The Darrell Survey

Frank Fenton

I am sure you have been wondering how so many different golf club companies can claim to be "number one" in the ads you see. They can't all be right. Someone has to be number two or three or four, right? Well, it all depends on how you measure popularity. Next time you see a print ad, look at the small print at the bottom of the page and you will get your answer.

Some companies back their "number one" claim with unit sales for a determined period of time. They are really saying that they sell a lot of sets of clubs—but it may be at lower prices than their competitors. Other companies go by sales dollars for a determined period. This may mean that they sell fewer clubs at higher prices, so their sales figures are larger than their competitor's. The time period they select may be to their advantage—possibly a particularly strong sales quarter in their fiscal year.

However, most of these ads quote something called the Darrell Survey. The Darrell Survey is an actual count of what the Tour players are using on any given week at a Tour event. The people from the Darrell Survey Company (a market research company) show up at the event and check each pro's equipment and clothing before each player tees off for the first round of competition (Thursdays for the PGA Tour and LPGA Tour, Fridays for the Senior Tour). The people from the Darrell Survey, from co-owner John Minkley to the on-the-road employees, go around with their clipboards and note exactly what kind of drivers, fairway woods, irons, wedges, putters, balls, shafts, grips, shoes, gloves, shirts, hats, bags, and sometimes even pants and socks, pro players are using and wearing.

As you know, many pros are paid hefty sums of cash to endorse and promote certain brands of clubs and clothes. The Darrell Survey is an accurate way of keeping everyone honest in adhering to their contracts. The survey people sell the information they gather to golf companies so they can be sure their money is being spent well. Golf companies also use this valuable data to promote their products in their advertising—here's the creative part. A particular golf club may be the overwhelming choice of the pros one or more weeks on the Tour. A company has every right to tell you when this is so. Some companies, however, are only able to win the "count" by the Darrell Survey on very few occasions each year. This does not stop them from telling the world that they are "number one on Tour" in their ads. It's up to you to read the small print that says they were number one for the third week of July, for fairway woods, with stiff, steel shafts only. I am slightly exaggerating, but you get the point. Some cagey companies, knowing that they cannot compete financially with the very large golf companies, are clever enough to go out and "buy" the count a certain week of the year. They do this by putting all their Tour promo money up for grabs in one week, paying a larger-than-normal premium to players who switch to their product that week. Remember, the count is done the first day of competition, so the pros can collect the extra money for going through the count with the bonus club that week and then switch back to their truly favorite club for the rest of the tournament. I know this is hard to believe, but it does happen. After all, I have heard that these are *professional* golfers we are watching. They don't do this just for fun.

You can imagine the task it is to take an actual count from some of the pros. Let's say you are a pro and you suddenly, inexplicably, start hitting your tee shots sideways. Then, naturally, you may want to try a different driver. But if you were paid gobs of money to play the first driver, you may not be too happy about someone pulling off the head cover and writing down what driver you switched to when you know this information may jeopardize your contract with your generous benefactor. I have heard stories of pros keeping towels over their clubs and shooing away the Darrell Survey people to keep their club-switching a secret. This rarely works with the persistent Darrell Survey counters. Some players are paid to wear a certain type of the softer spikes but wear something else instead. The Darrell Survey people are so well trained that they wait until the player actually hits his tee ball and then note the spikes that are seen on the bottom of his shoes as he finishes his follow-through.

There are numerous people from golf companies at Tour events each week who go to great trouble and expense to build clubs for the pros to test and play. Companies like Callaway, Taylor Made, and Mizuno each have a full van at these events to make clubs up on the spot in hopes that players will use them and keep them through the Darrell Survey count.

All this effort by all these people to get the pros to use their products is great for advertising purposes, but I always say that the proof is in the pudding. If a club, shaft, or ball truly performs well, it won't take long for the golfing public to find out. The Darrell Survey merely gives golf companies the ammo to write the wonderful ads that help you become aware of new products that may help your game.

17

Wedge Fitting

Frank Fenton

Previously I discussed different drivers that you might try to better fit the characteristics of your own particular golf game. In this chapter I'll give you some tips on selecting a wedge or group of wedges for you to improve your scoring.

If you have been playing golf for many years, you may have noticed that you hit your pitching wedge (PW) longer than you used to. If you have purchased a set of irons in the last dozen years or so, you should understand that the PW that came with your newer set of irons is not the same as the older wedges. As iron lofts have been made stronger (i.e. with less loft) and the shaft lengths have increased, the distance that you hit a ball has gotten longer. Pitching wedges used to have loft angles of fifty to fifty-two degrees. Nowadays PWs have loft angles of forty-seven to forty-nine degrees. Golf club designers are always looking to give you more distance, and this is one of the ways they do it. They also want to entice better players to use these modern irons that have cavity backs and low center of gravity locations. The lower lofts help to bring the ball flight down. In any event, you hit a newer PW farther than an older one. That's one wedge you need.

The loft of the sand wedge (SW) in your set has remained relatively the same over the years, about fifty-five to fifty-seven degrees. This spec was kept so you still could have sufficient loft to get the ball out of a greenside sand bunker. You may have already guessed that if the PW loft got stronger and the SW loft stayed the same, a yardage problem may occur. You are right. Unless you are a wizard with taking some distance off your PW shots or powering your SW distance, you will have a gap in the comfortable distances that you hit these clubs. Let's say that you hit your PW 110 yards in the air. Let's also say that you carry your SW eighty-five yards. You need something that you can easily swing and carry the ball around ninety-five to a hundred yards. This is why many golf companies now offer a "gap" wedge to match their sets or to be sold as an extra utility club. They are also sometimes called "mid-wedge" or "approach wedge." In any case, these clubs have between fifty-one and fifty-four degrees loft. If you don't have one of these, and you have trouble with that in-between yardage, you should consider getting one. That's two wedges.

The sand wedge you choose should be playable in the conditions in which you use it most often. Many golfers use the SW from the fairway and rough and to chip with around the green. If this is your case, you may want a SW with a standard loft but with less sole bounce than most sand wedges normally have.

The sole bounce is the angle on the bottom part of the club head. This angle is called "bounce" if the rear part of the sole is lower than the part of the sole near the leading edge of the club. You can see it if you hold the club head up at eye level, with the end of the toe facing you. The greater the sole bounce, the less the sole bottom will dig into the sand when you hit a bunker shot. This is good if you play golf on a course that has a lot of sand or fluffy sand in the bunkers. If the sand is hard-packed or there is just not much of it in the bunkers, you may want to try a SW with less bounce. A SW with too much bounce hit from hard-packed sand or firm turf can cause the SW club head to skip into the ball, causing a sculled shot over the green. That's three wedges.

There are many shots close to the green that you may be unable to hit with the first three wedges I've discussed. Suppose that you have a shot of forty yards over a pond to an elevated, hard green. Or suppose you are faced with a shot from a deep greenside bunker with a high lip and little green to work with. What do you do? The lob wedge is perfect for these types of shots and others. The lob wedge has from fifty-eight to sixty-four degrees of loft. If you don't already have one, I would suggest you get one soon. Most PGA Tour players carry something in this range. This is how they hit those wonderful shots around the greens that stop on a dime, right next to the hole. I have found that many amateur golfers would benefit from using a more lofted wedge from the sand around the greens. It is much easier to get the ball up out of the sand and then stop it quickly with a sixty-degree wedge. Give this a try. Just be sure that the lob wedge you choose is playable from the sand and the grass. If the sole is wide enough not to dig into the sand and the bounce angle is not so great as to make the sole of the club head bounce off the turf, you have found a good lob wedge. That's four wedges. That's enough. Have fun experimenting and see which wedges best help your game.

18

Golfers Should Hit Balls, Not the Bottle

David Grimes

A writer has suggested that professional golf could be made more exciting if the players were required to drink one or more shots of Scotch whisky per hole. Robert Mackey, of the online magazine *Slate*, is of the opinion that modern golf, at least as it's played by Tiger Woods and company, has lost touch with its roots and become dull and predictable.

"Hitting a dimpled ball with a machine-tooled wedge one hundred yards to within ten feet of a hole in a pedicured green from a perfect lie on a fairway mowed to precisely 1.6 inches and through bone-dry, windless air is one kind of accomplishment," Mackey writes. "Knocking a big pebble one hundred paces through a howling gale and a driving rain from a tangle of weeds to within a few inches of a sheep's turd is quite another."

"She's driving me to golf!"

Mackey claims that the only way our golfing ancestors, the Scots, could endure the wretched game was to get thoroughly plastered. The game was standardized at eighteen holes, he says, because there are thirty-six shots of whiskey in a bottle. (Lucky for all that the modern bottle of 1.75 liters had not yet come on the scene, or a round of golf would take even longer than it does today.) While Mackey's argument does have some merit (it would be amusing to watch the pros' skills steadily deteriorate during the course of a round, just like amateurs' do), I can see some potential problems.

At a professional tournament, it might not be a good thing for the pros to be more inebriated than the fans watching them. It is one thing for excessively exuberant fans to throw cups of beer at Tiger Woods when he makes a hole in one; it would be another thing entirely for Tiger, after making a quadruple-bogey nine, to wade into the crowd and smash a bottle of Johnnie Walker over someone's head.

It is true that the golf pros on TV often appear excessively stiff and seldom have anything more interesting to say than that they "stayed focused" or "played their own game." A pro who had just downed twenty or thirty shots of Scotch would surely be more voluble, if not necessarily comprehensible. There is also the very real possibility of players passing out on the tees or greens, slowing play or, at the very least, making for some awkward lies.

I suspect that golf course superintendents would also disapprove of this change in the rules. Golf courses suffer enough damage from weekend hackers without the best players in the world taking drunken chops and gouges out of the fairways and greens and leaving the place looking like an abandoned phosphate mine.

There is also the possibility that some pros would play better with a few pops under their belt. (This is a not uncommon phenomenon in the amateur ranks.) Others, unused to consuming anything stronger than Perrier, might find themselves unable to compete and would have to pursue other, less glamorous lines of work, such as selling bait or writing humor columns.

Finally, golf is a gentleman's game, at least in theory. All that would surely go out the window if the players were consuming excessive quantities of alcohol. Rules disagreements would be settled by an eight iron to the head rather than by calling in an official. Scoring disputes would also escalate when players got to the point where they couldn't remember if they got a ten or a thirteen on the previous hole.

Professional golfers make the game look ridiculously easy, and it would be nice to handicap them in some way so that their games more closely resembled ours. Filling them full of booze may not be the answer, but making them knock a large pebble toward a sheep turd has definite possibilities.

19

Payne Stewart

Frank Fenton

This was not the story I had planned on writing that week. But I was abruptly informed that our 1999 U.S. Open champion, Payne Stewart, had just died in a plane crash. I knew that by the time my article was published it would be very old news—every network was spending plenty of time on the story. But as I heard the unwelcome report, all I could think about was the young player I had met at the beginning of 1979.

I had just started to work with Dave Pelz, now known as a famous short game instructor to the Tour stars and a familiar face on the Golf Channel. We ran a small putter company in Maryland, and Dave was only beginning to make his reputation as a putting teacher with some of the PGA Tour players. We had driven the company's old van from Maryland to the PGA Merchandise Show in Orlando, Florida, and from there to Dallas, Texas, to attend the Ad Specialty Show. We had discovered that selling six putters at a time to golf shops would not make us rich, so we had a line of putters that other companies would buy from us, put their logos on, and give away as promotional items. We were to meet up with a fellow by the name of Herb Durham in Dallas. Herb was a top ad specialty salesman in the area and an avid golfer. He belonged to Preston Trail Country Club, where the Byron Nelson Tour event was played for many years. Herb asked us to join him for a game at his club. He brought with him a good-looking young man who, we were told, was the captain of the Southern Methodist University (SMU) golf team.

As we ate a quick breakfast, the young man from SMU mentioned that he had heard that I had been a golf pro. He said that he too would like to be a pro. Thinking that he was referring to a job as a club professional (which I had been), I wished him luck and told him to expect to work many long hours. He clarified that he was planning on playing golf professionally. "Oh," I said. "Well, practice hard because that's a very difficult profession that only a few guys can really do well at." Sound advice, I thought, from an older and wiser man (I was only four years older).

The day was one of those cold raw days that you can get in Dallas in early February. We played anyway, and the young man from SMU hit the ball pretty well, considering the conditions. We sat over warm drinks and the young fella said that if he could learn to putt the ball a little better he just might have a chance on the Tour. We all spent the next hour going over some of the finer points of putting. I remember how excited the young guy was when Dave gave him some tips that seemed to work. Herb remarked to us what a fine young man the guy was, what a great personality he had, and not to worry about him. "If he doesn't make it as a golfer, I have already offered him a job with me selling ad specialty products," he said. A PGA Championship and a couple of U.S. Opens later, we all knew that we didn't have to worry about him. Can you imagine Payne Stewart selling logo pens and coffee mugs? I can. He would have made you glad that you bought from him. He was that kind of guy.

As the years went on, I would run into Payne from time to time out on the Tour. We were not really close, but I knew him well enough to say hello and talk occasionally. He always made you pleased that you spoke with him. The week before he passed away, I had just seen him on the range at the National Car Rental Golf Classic at Disney World. He was incognito with his long pants and baseball cap. Out on Tour most weeks the Professional Tour Caddie Association has a trailer that is taken from event to event. Since the caddies are generally not permitted in the clubhouse, the trailer is there for them to eat in and get out of the hot sun. One of the best-kept secrets is that many of the Tour players and pro-motional people also eat in this trailer. It is a very informal, lunch-eonette type of deal. As I ate my lunch in there that Wednesday, I looked over across the trailer and there was Payne. He was not an ostentatious guy. He may have dressed that way for the spectators, but only to be a little different from the rest of the players and give the fans something interesting to see. He had won the U.S. Open and over $2 million that year, but he had chosen to eat with the guys in the trailer.

When I heard of his passing, I checked the latest PGA Tour stats. Payne was number two in putting and putts per round. It looks like all that practice paid off. Life is short. Play hard.

20

Strange Tour Tales

Frank Fenton

Whenile I watched Tiger Woods on TV make U.S. Open history at Pebble Beach in June of 2000, I noticed that they showed the famous *Life* magazine photo of Ben Hogan. I'm sure that you have seen this picture of Hogan hitting the #1 iron to the eighteenth green at Merion in the 1950 Open. Mr. Hogan had won the 1948 Open and was unable to defend his title in 1949 after being nearly killed in a terrible accident in which a bus hit his car head on. They played 36 holes on the last day back in 1950, and Hogan was just about wore out from walking on his still-suffering legs. Mr. Hogan had told us that he was just trying to get the ball on the green so that he could two-putt for par. With this accomplished, he was able to get in a playoff the next day with 1946 Open champ Lloyd Mangrum and George Fazio. Hogan beat them by four shots to claim his second official U.S. Open.

There is a somewhat strange tale about the famous club used to hit this notable shot at Merion. After the 1950 Open win, Mr. Hogan was playing in an event and left his bag of clubs resting against the bag rail outside the clubhouse. When he came out to retrieve his clubs, the #1 iron was missing. It was gone for over thirty years. One day in 1983, Lanny Wadkins (who was a Hogan staff player at the time) was approached by a guy at the Players Championship who dealt in old, classic clubs. He showed the iron to Lanny and they agreed that the vintage MacGregor club must have belonged to Hogan. Mr. Hogan played MacGregor clubs before starting his own club company in 1953. Irons of that era had long hosels, and good players quickly realized that the true "sweet spot" (center of gravity) was in toward the hosel. A perfectly struck shot had to be almost shanked, and this particular club had a small worn area, the size of a quarter, slightly in towards the heel side of the center of the club face. A truly skilled golfer must have owned this club. Lanny brought it into the Hogan plant. After reviewing it, Mr. Hogan felt it was his long-lost club.

Gene Sheeley (Mr. Hogan's personal club-maker and the man who taught me club design) brought the club down to our research and development shop. There, Gene and I cleaned it up, removed the more modern green "Victory" grip, and replaced it with a cord grip like those Mr. Hogan used. Gene even went through the trouble of putting a string cord reminder rib under the grip, cocked to the 5:30 position, just like Mr. Hogan played. This was done with an old wooden jig that had been made up so that each rib would be positioned to Mr. Hogan's personal specs. This famous club is now on display in the Ben Hogan Room at the USGA Golf House museum in Far

Hills, New Jersey. If you are ever in the area, be sure to stop by and see this great treasury of golf items.

From another "Strange But True" file comes this short tale of former Senior PGA Tour player Dick Rhyan. Dick recently had laser eye surgery and no longer needs to wear his contact lenses during play. But it seems that some years back (around '95 or '96 as Dick remembers it), he was playing in a Senior Tour event at Piper Glen in North Carolina and was wearing his contacts ("was" being the operative word here). As he walked up on the tee box, Dick noticed that his right eye didn't feel quite right. He kept blinking, feeling that perhaps the contact lens wasn't sitting properly. He hit his drive off into the rough, but it was playable. As he stood over his approach shot, he kept blinking. And then it happened. The lens was gone. He looked all over his shirt, pants, shoes, and the deep grass with no luck. Now he was one-eyed and without a back-up lens in his bag, only a small bottle of lens solution. Rhyan called for a tournament official. "Could you please contact my wife and ask her to get over here right away with my other contacts," he said. The official agreed to his request, but told Dick he must continue to play so as to not hold up the field.

Rhyan squinted at the ball in the rough and took a swipe at it. With his one-eyed attempt he was only able to get the ball up near the green. He chipped his next shot on the putting surface. As he bent down to mark his ball, he saw it: the slightly blue tint of the lens. It was stuck to the ball cover as if on an eyeball. The lens had already begun to dry like a decal on the ball, and was stuck on the cover well enough to stay on for the long ride of his second shot as well as the chip shot. This is incredible when you think about all the distortion and revolutions the golf ball goes through when it is struck. Now, Dick was playing for a lot of money in this event, and anyone who knows him knows that he doesn't like to waste money. So what does he do? He floods the golf ball lens with contact lens solution and removes it from the ball. After it is soaked in his palm for a short period it looks okay, so he pops it back into his eye. He can see fine and proceeds to finish the round, shooting a nice 69. End of story.

21

The Grimes Guide to Golf Bets

(or How to Press a Nassau Without Getting Skinned)

David Grimes

I have heard it said that there are people who play golf for the fresh air and the exercise. I have also heard it said that there are hairy, eight-foot-tall creatures living in the foothills of the Himalayas. Who knows, maybe they're one and the same. But until I meet one I'm going to have to go with the assumption that most golfers like to have a small wager going while they're playing. It gets the blood pumping, focuses the mind, and gives you something to argue about on the first tee.

First, let us make a distinction here between wagering and gambling. Wagering is something done between the players. You are betting on yourself or your team. If you lose, you should be unhappy, but not to the point that you don't know how you're going to make your next house payment. Gambling, on the other hand, is evil and insidious and scary, and if you're caught doing it, they can keep you out of the Hall of Fame. Or worse. A good rule of thumb is that if you have to buy the first round of drinks, you're wagering. If there's a beefy guy named Vito waiting in the parking lot to collect his money, you're gambling.

This article will focus on golf wagering, of which there are many kinds. Some of the games are so complicated you need an accountant to keep track. If you are new to golf, I suggest you stay away from these games. In fact, if you're new to golf, I suggest you stay away from wagering altogether unless you enjoy losing.

If your playing partners are trying to suck you into a game with which you are unfamiliar, it is a good idea to ask this question: How much can I possibly lose? In some games it's impossible to tell how much you can lose because the amount of the bet varies (invariably upward) during the course of the round. Stay away from these games unless you are carrying a big wad of cash or have an extraordinary amount of confidence in your ability or you're getting a lot of strokes. Someone once said that all bets are won or lost on the first tee and I have seen no evidence in thirty-five years of playing that contradicts that statement. In a perfect world, all players would have honest handicaps and the strokes would be assigned thereby. (A twelve-handicapper playing a six-handicapper would get a stroke subtracted from his score on each of the six hardest holes. In other words, if the twelve-handicapper got a five and the other golfer got a four, the hole would be tied.)

But this is not a perfect world, which means that strokes are assigned according to what you can get away with. The first tee is the place to mention your bad back, the heat, the cold, or how the alignment of the planets Mars and Jupiter has negatively affected your biorhythms. Whatever it takes to get you that precious extra stroke or two, otherwise known as the "edge." If you are getting strokes, know on what holes they fall. In fact, it's a good idea to circle them on your scorecard. Since these holes are among the toughest, a bogey-net-par will often be good enough to win. Play these holes smartly, which is to say conservatively. Shoot away from the water, trees, or out-of-bounds stakes. Increase your chances of hitting the fairway by taking a three-wood off the tee instead of a driver. Go for the middle of the green.

This works so well that you may come to the conclusion that this is the proper way to play every hole, and it is, with the possible exception of Skins. Skins is the best betting game there is because you can play like a dog all day but have one good hole and win all the money. Skins is also the worst betting game there is because you can play great for eighteen holes and not win a dime.

To play skins, the first thing you do is set the stakes. If you decide to play for $1 a hole, the most you can win or lose on the day is $18. The skin goes to the player with the lowest score on the hole. If two or more players tie, the skin is carried over to the next hole, which is now worth $2. Another tie, the next hole is worth $3, etc. Even if you've been playing like a goat all day, you could, theoretically, find yourself playing the last hole for $18.

This might be a good time to let it all hang out and play the hole aggressively. Then again, if your opponents all snap-hook it into the cabbage, a more conservative line of play may be indicated. Good luck.

Golfers who aren't playing skins are usually playing a team game called best-ball or foursomes (four-ball in the U.K.). You

**"Can you spare two dollars,
I haven't hit a golf ball in weeks"**

and your partner try to beat the tar out of the other two guys. Low score on each side is the score for the team. Most games are match-play, which means each hole is a separate match. If you beat the other team by one stroke or ten strokes, you're still only one up. If you win the next hole, you're two up. If the other team wins the next hole, then you go back to one up on the eighteen-hole match. It is possible, in match play, to have a higher score than the other team and win.

Many best-ball games are played as a nassau. This has nothing to do with the city in the Bahamas except that it's a form of wagering. You play for three points: front nine, back nine and total for the eighteen. If you and your partner finish the front nine one-up, then you win the front-nine point and whatever dollar amount you've assigned to it. You are also one-up on the eighteen, with the back-nine still to play. If you lose the back-nine two-down, your opponents win the back-nine point and win the overall eighteen one-up. That means they have two points to your one. If you're playing a $5 nassau, your opponents walk away with $5 each, unless of course, there's been . . .

A press. During the first-tee negotiations, you might hear something like: Five dollar nassau and two-down automatics. This has nothing to do with rapid-fire weapons. (Unless, of course, Vito is waiting for you in the parking lot.) What it means is that as soon as either team falls to two-down, another $5 bet automatically begins. That second bet is called a "press."

The first thing you need to know about presses is that they can quickly add up. Let's say you're two-down and a press has kicked in. You get nervous and before you know it, you're four-down on the original bet and two-down on the press. Because you're two-down on the press, another press automatically kicks in. If you lose the next hole, you're five-down on the original bet, three-down on the first press and one-down on the second press. You are now staring at a $15 loss (or more because you're five-down in the overall match) and you haven't even made it to the back nine. In the worst-case scenario, meaning that you and your partner lose every hole, the innocent-sounding $5 nassau suddenly, not to mention tragically, has you reaching in your pocket for $55. Next time you'll know to beg for more strokes on the first tee. And even more importantly, you'll know to find yourself a better partner.

22

More Mr. Hogan and the Colonial

Frank Fenton

F ort Worth, Texas, was my home for nearly five years when I ran golf club research and development at the Ben Hogan Company in the mid- to late 1980s. Each May, when "Colonial Week" came around, it was like your birthday and the Fourth of July rolled into one glorious week of golfing bliss. Mr. Hogan was alive and well at that time, and if you worked with him at his namesake golf company you were treated very well during Colonial Week. Of course, the event is known as the Bank of America Colonial now, but back then it was the Colonial National Invitation Tournament and was regarded by the PGA Tour players as a very prestigious event to win. I'm sure that it still is today, but in years past it was close to the level of a major. Some of this is due to Mr. Hogan's record as a five-time champion in 1946, '47, '52, '53 and '59. Some of it is from the way the tournament was run, by invitation only. In any event, the players, especially the Hogan staff players, wouldn't miss a chance to play in the Colonial.

Each year Mr. Hogan and his wife, Valerie, would host a dinner at Shady Oaks Country Club, where Mr. Hogan was, of course, the most noted member. The Tour players on the Hogan staff and a very small group of the people from the Hogan Company who interacted with the players (in regards to equipment, contracts and so forth) would be invited to this wonderful affair. I recall that the Hogans always presented our wives with some sort of small, elegant gift—a touch of class from days gone by. Dining and talking with players such as Larry Nelson, Gil Morgan, Lanny Wadkins, the very quiet and polite Mike Reid and Jack Renner, and some up-and-coming rookies, Mark O'Meara and Nick Price, was a true delight.

Each year different people at the Hogan Company would take a turn at playing in the pro-am. I played soon after I had arrived in Texas, and though I was a low-handicap player at the time, I must confess that playing in the famous Fort Worth wind to the hard and fast Colonial greens took its toll on me that day. I did make a birdie in front of a large gallery on the par-four ninth over the water. The crowd cheered, I felt great, and the rest of the day didn't psychologically scar me too badly. I really understood the feelings of the other Hogan people who played in the years following that. Just trying not to hurt anyone in the crowd and play halfway decent golf was a good day. But, man was it fun.

I have attended most of the recent Colonials and as I watched a few of the groups go by in the pro-ams I could really empathize with some of the amateurs. Not all of them mind you, only the ones who looked like they understood and could play the game somewhat, but were having a little bit of the jitters. Some pro-am participants at every Tour event are not ready for a big gallery and shouldn't be subjected to such terror until they are able to raise their skill level and knowledge of the game. I saw one guy have his caddie get down in the sand with him to take his picture as he executed his bunker shot. Delay of game, five yard penalty. I think that these guys get roped into playing in a pro-am because their boss insisted that they do so or a well-meaning wife gave them their spot as an anniversary gift. Oh well.

I always enjoy going to the Colonial to see the people: well-dressed business men with their shiny shoes and ties sneaking out for a long lunch to catch a little of the golfing action; their well-coifed wives with their jewelry and high heels (really not the attire for following your favorite pro around the course); the happy, loud-talking Fort Worthians with their white straw cowboy hats, jeans and boots; and the standard spectator for all Tour events decked out in a Polo shirt, Gap khaki shorts, and new white sneakers. This crowd mixes together well and all have a good time.

Not long ago Colonial spent $3.25 million making a few changes to the course such as rebuilding the greens, lengthening some holes, and adding or stretching some bunkers in key locations. The greens in past years have been very fast (one player told me U.S. Open speed, 11 to 11.5 on the Stimpmeter) and very hard (not uncommon for Texas greens when the wind blows as it does in Fort Worth). The greens, cut short for the tournament, would very often dry up and die by the Monday following the event, leaving the members to play to temporary greens until the damage could be repaired. Lately, though the greens have been great. Nice green grass, not too hard, and rolling true at about 10.5.

The players have by now figured out that some of the bunkers have been enlarged to catch some shots that in years past would have carried the sand easily. Most notable is the dogleg left, long par-four third hole. This hole used to require a big draw around the corner, with the left side protected by a few bunkers. The players had gotten so good over the years that they would just aim their tee shots up and over the tall trees on the left and carry all the traps, leaving them a short iron into the green. The new elongated bunkers should discourage some of that. To carry up the left side now will require a huge tee ball. Fail to fly the bunkers and they will be faced with a very difficult shot out of a semi-deep sand trap to the green. Good luck, boys.

On my last trip to Colonial I went into the clubhouse lobby to see one of my favorite displays, the Hogan Trophy Room, just to the right through the front doors. It has been completely redone and is now called the Ben Hogan Memorial Room. I must say that they did a nice job. Tom Kite popped in for a quick review while I was there and seemed pleased. There is an interactive video display to give you some of the history of Mr. Hogan's accomplishments, and some interviews with him. I liked the part in which a very serious Ken Venturi asked Mr. Hogan if he ever thought that he would be able to come back to the level he was before the near deadly car accident in 1949. Mr. Hogan's firm, one word reply, "Yes." He did go on to explain why, but that "yes" was priceless.

In this room you can see many of the irons from the Ben Hogan Company I'm proud to say that the 1988 Apex iron I designed is in there. Most, however, were done by Mr. Hogan's right hand man and master club builder, Gene Sheeley. Also in the room you'll see trophies from Mr. Hogan's victories at the Masters, PGA, British Open and four U.S. Opens. There are, however, five identical USGA medallions there. Mr. Hogan won a national open, with a first class field, run (at least in part) by the USGA in 1942. Due to a matter known as World War II, this was not an official U.S. Open according to the USGA. Mr. Hogan privately felt that this was indeed his first National Open (what the U.S. Open was then called) and in his eyes, his fifth U.S. Open. After the war, he won the Open in 1948, '50, '51 and '53. What is truly amazing is that after he was almost killed in 1949 when his auto was crushed by an oncoming bus in Van Horn, Texas, he won the Open at Merion in 1950!

In this room at Colonial is a flagstick from the eighteenth hole at Merion with its famous basket top instead of a flag (no help with the wind from these things). Mr. Hogan's Open win in 1953 went along that same year with wins at the Masters and his one and only trip to the British Open at Carnoustie in Scotland. A photo hangs in this room that shows Mr. Hogan sitting in a shiny open top black car going down the street in New York City during his ticker tape parade. This is what presidents and astronauts received. That I actually knew someone who had such a parade still boggles my mind.

Not on display at Colonial are some of the original, priceless trophies and awards like the Masters clubhouse trophy and the Hickok Belt awarded to him for being the top professional athlete in 1953. These items are on display at the World Golf Hall of Fame. The old Hogan Trophy Room at Colonial was broken into before and some of these cherished effects were stolen by obvious non-golf fans who tried to hock the stones. Mr. Hogan felt that more people would be able to see these items at the Hall of

Fame and the security there would be tighter.

Once, early during Colonial week, I walked outside by the eighteenth green and saw the big scoreboard facing the grand-stands. Since the actual competition hadn't started and no Tour players were listed on the board yet, the names of past champi-ons were there instead with the years that they had won the event. Names like "Watson," "Frost," and "Price." And was the name at the very top "Hogan"? No way—it was *"Mr.* Hogan" who topped the list. It's how we all referred to him when I worked at his company and it's how the people of Fort Worth still refer to him. I looked back up the eighteenth fairway and I noticed that the big old oak tree that used to overhang the left side of the fairway was no longer there. I'm sure someone told me that it fell down or something. The hole looks too easy with no tree guarding that left side. I did notice that the fairway looked a lit-tle narrower and a new small oak was planted right at that left edge. In a few years, that tree will grow and the branches will make a sterner test of that hole. Mr. Hogan wouldn't have it any other way.

23

Gene Sheeley

Frank Fenton

Although I had already spent seven years in the golf business as a golf professional, plant manager, and production superintendent for other golf companies, I really began my education in the golf club design and development business in 1983 when I started work at the Ben Hogan Company. There are very few true craftsman golf club designers in the business. I was fortunate enough to have worked with one of the best.

Gene Sheeley had started his vocation in the golf business as an apprentice for the Kenneth Smith Golf Company (one of the premier custom club builders of that era) in the late 1930s in Kansas City, Missouri. He began his education working on hickory shafted clubs and learning how to sand the shafts to create the proper feel and kick point that was required for the particular golfer he was fitting.

When World War II came along Gene enlisted in the Navy. The destroyer he was assigned to collided with another ship and sank. Gene was lucky to escape with his life. After the war he returned to Kansas City to continue his work at Kenneth Smith. When the Korean War started, Gene once again enlisted, this time in the Marines. He saw action in Korea and was wounded in the arm. After recuperating, he was assigned to duty in New Orleans where he met his wife-to-be. Following his hitch in the Marines he went back to work for Kenneth Smith.

In 1964, Ben Hogan was interviewing people to work in the golf club development area of his golf company. I am sure that Gene's tenacity toward life and his strong work ethic was a big factor in Mr. Hogan hiring Gene. When these two met, a lifelong bond was forged. For the next thirty-plus years Gene Sheeley was at Mr. Hogan's side when it came time to discuss new club designs. Gene—with Mr. Hogan's approval—was the designer of all the early classic Apex irons from the 1960s up to the 1980s.

I spent almost my first full year at Hogan working by Gene's side trying to absorb as much information and technique as I could. Gene, like many of the craftsman club-makers, did not quantify his method of designing and blending a set of clubs together into a cohesive unit. He used the skill of his hands and eyes and his many years of just doing this work to decide when a set of irons was complete. My method was to not only develop a "good eye" for clubs, but also develop a method using mathematics and trigonometry to create a set of clubs that, as Gene would say, were all "brothers." After I had spent over four years learning from and working with Gene and Mr. Hogan, I was fortunate enough to have been given the task of creating the BH88 Apex irons, which were designed and developed in 1987. This blade was subsequently used as the basis for the next several Apex iron modifications and remains in use on the PGA Tour today. Gene continued on with the Hogan Company working on the Hogan Edge and GCD irons toward the end of his career.

Gene Sheeley was a tough old guy and as long as I knew him he had an unfiltered cigarette in his mouth. Even after his voice began to get rough, he still had that cigarette dangling from his lips. This eventually caught up with him. He was one of the very few people who called Mr. Hogan "Ben." I believe that Gene would have done anything for Mr. Hogan, and certainly his many years of loyal service were proof of that. I was not surprised to hear that after Mr. Hogan passed away in July 1997, Gene was not far behind him. I'm sure he felt that after Mr. Hogan was gone his mission on earth was complete and it was okay to rest.

I remember the last time that I saw Gene was right before I left the Hogan Company to start work at Spalding. We played golf together at Gene's club, Glen Garden in Fort Worth, Texas. This is the same club where two young boys named Ben Hogan and Byron Nelson learned to caddie and play the game of golf. I remember winning a dollar from Gene that day and I asked him to sign it for me, which he did. I need to find that dollar. I know that I kept it and it's around here somewhere. It is a link with the past and a memento from a great club-maker. It should be framed and on the wall.

24

How I Survived Spiro Agnew

David Grimes

A recent story in the *Los Angeles Times* asserted that golf is not the gentlemanly game it once was. The story included real-life examples of golfers beating each other up, hitting balls at one another, and otherwise exhibiting the kind of surly behavior you might expect to find at an English soccer match or American Little League game.

The story reminded me of the time I was almost killed by Spiro Agnew, the disgraced and dearly departed ex-vice president under disgraced and dearly departed Richard Nixon.

I was playing with a friend at an Ocean City, Maryland, course that Agnew liked to play when he was in town. We were lining up our birdie putts on a short par three when a ball dropped from the sky, landing between the hole and me. I turned toward the tee and saw Agnew standing with a club in his hand and a disgusted look on his face.

"Damn the luck!" he seemed to be saying. "I had a clear shot at a young, left-leaning journalist and I missed him! Quick! Hand me another bribe . . . er, ball and let me try again!"

I had several options at this point. I could pretend nothing had happened and finish putting. This didn't seem like a good idea as it would give Agnew time to reload and perhaps improve his aim.

Another option was to tee up his ball and smack it back at him with my putter. This seemed unwise for several reasons. Number One, the shot was about 150 yards long, which called for a seven-iron rather than a putter. By the time I went back to my bag and fetched the right club, the moment would be lost. Number Two, I was badly shaken, meaning that I was more likely to mis-hit the shot, possibly taking a deep gouge out of the green, than I was of zipping one past Agnew's ear. This would only lower myself and my generation farther in his esteem, if such a thing were possible. Third, and most importantly, Agnew was playing with three other men, all beefy Secret-Service types in dark sunglasses who probably had Uzis in their golf bags, if not shoulder-fired nuclear missiles, that they were itching to try out on two long-haired young people who had the audacity to nearly impede the forward progress of the vice president's golf ball with their heads.

So I elected response Number Four: I picked up my golf ball (giving myself the birdie putt, of course) and walked (briskly) to the next tee.

It is an anti-climactic ending, I admit, but I think it's instructive in its own pathetic way. Just because someone else is a jerk doesn't mean you have to be one, too. This is as true on the golf course as it is on the road, in the movie theater or in the living

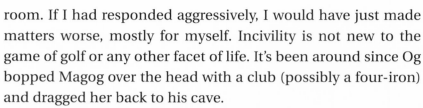

room. If I had responded aggressively, I would have just made matters worse, mostly for myself. Incivility is not new to the game of golf or any other facet of life. It's been around since Og bopped Magog over the head with a club (possibly a four-iron) and dragged her back to his cave.

I like to think that Agnew eventually felt sorry for what he did. (Though Agnew had so many things to feel sorry about it's unlikely he ever got around to this particular incident.) But even if he didn't, I have the satisfaction of knowing that I did not contribute to the de-civilizing of the gentlemanly game of golf that summer day, so long ago.

And if my foot accidentally kicked Agnew's ball into the sand trap as I left the green, it wasn't because I was being malicious; I was just in a hurry.

25

Pro-grade versus Commercial-grade Clubs

Frank Fenton

Some golfers want no more than an attractive-looking set of new clubs to go out and bludgeon the ball across the fields and meadows of their local links. But if you want to have a set of matched precision instruments to skillfully play this game at the lowest scores possible, then you need to own pro-grade clubs.

There are numerous ways to tell the difference. One of the most obvious ways is the name recognition derived from the constant barrage of expensive advertisements. Big-name companies are very often pro-grade club producers, but not always. Just because some club company has a well-known logo or has a prominent pro endorse its clubs doesn't mean that the clubs are the quality that you may be led to believe. I know that this may be hard to accept, but there are some pros who, for the right amount of money, will endorse almost anything.

Thankfully, this is the exception rather than the rule. Always look at the quality of the clubs before you go by someone's paid endorsement. It is true that most pro-line club manufacturers have some type of pro recommendation. There are, however, some very good clubs out there that do not use this type of product advertising (or the company may be so new/small that it is not yet able to pay the hefty sums required for these types of endorsements). Also there are custom clubs that are made from high-quality individual components that, when assembled by skilled club-makers, will yield a pro-grade club.

The main difference between the pro-grade and commercial-grade clubs is the specifications of the components. For a pro-grade club, the head, shaft, and grip will be made from tried-and-true materials by skilled companies that are capable of producing such items. Let's break these down.

The head should be designed by people who know and understand the game of golf. It should be tested, not only by a robot, but by golfers who are in the target audience of that club (i.e., high-handicap golfers, better players, pros, etc.). Too many clubs are designed by engineers who have never swung a club. The multitude of situations that arise during a round of golf (different lies, trajectories required, depth of rough, etc.) must be considered and built into each club in a pro-grade set. A commercial-grade set may not address all these things. The lie angles should smoothly progress throughout the set, as should the loft angles and sole angles. The profiles of each head should blend into the shape of the next club in the set. The weight distribution of each head ought to be balanced to allow the correct center of gravity location required for that particular head. The materials the head is made from should be durable, strong and functional. A steel metal wood head or iron must be made from a quality stainless steel, never a zinc die cast material (though zinc is okay for a properly designed putter, the stress on a metal wood or an iron during play may cause the head to break). If the metal wood head is to be oversize and made of Titanium, then it should be made from the grade of Ti that performs the best, not just something with a little Ti powder sprinkled in for good luck. We are looking for precise equipment to play this game, not a miss-matched set of garden tools.

The shaft must be of the correct weight, length, torque, flex, and kick point to allow that individual club to do its best job. The shaft weight tolerance has to be tight to achieve the proper balance and swing weight that is best for that club. The shaft must provide the proper feedback through feel to the golfer to give him confidence that the shot he is attempting to hit can be done. Commercial-grade clubs' shafts may be made to wide tolerances that create more doubt, rather than confidence, in your swing. Graphite shafts need to be made from the high-quality fibers that produce a strong, consistent shaft. Don't be fooled by incredibly low-priced graphite shafts. Chances are they were really designed to be umbrella handles or fishing rods rather than golf club shafts.

The grips should be made of durable materials that are resistant to the ozone and the sun's ultraviolet rays. If you see a new set of clubs and the grips are already getting slick or are "blooming" (the whitish powder is forming on the surface), be sure to pass on these clubs. The grips should be of uniform size and weight throughout the set. Commercial grips can be of varying sizes, causing you to slice one club and hook the next due to your hands being on the club differently. Too small of a grip and your hands can get overactive, causing a hook; too large and you may be unable to release the club head, resulting in a slice. If the weights of the grips are inconsistent, the overall weight and balance of the clubs may be thrown off.

The method of assembly is even different for pro grade versus commercial grade. Some large club manufacturers offer both lines of clubs to the public at different prices. Sometimes these two different grades of clubs are being built in the same factory. If this is the case, you can bet that a different set of manufacturing instructions and specifications are being used. If a set of clubs is to be sold for a lower price, then corners must be cut—not only on the materials, but on the methods of assembly as well. For example, they may not set the loft or lie as well as they should. They may skip the extra screw that holds everything securely together, the grips may not be lined up as well, the balance points or swing weights may be ignored, and so on.

Don't get me wrong. There are many people who would just as soon own a set of the cheaper, commercial-grade clubs. They will get all the performance they need from these lower-cost clubs since they are just out to beat the ball around and enjoy the weather. But if you want to really play this game and you have the desire to improve and score your absolute best, then you must be willing to make the investment in top-quality, pro-grade clubs.

26

Grooves

Frank Fenton

few years ago there were a lot of words flying back and forth between the United States Golf Association (USGA) and some of the golf club manufacturers and the PGA Tour regarding grooves. The USGA felt that some of the companies were pushing the boundaries of the Rules of Golf set forth by the USGA and The Royal and Ancient of St. Andrews. (The R&A generally writes the rules for the rest of the world in conjunction with the USGA standards.) When all this happened, exhaustive tests were conducted with machines and live golfers to determine what effect these grooves had on golf shots hit from various conditions.

Some golf companies were making their grooves with a radius slightly too large on the groove edge where the groove wall meets the face plane of the club. This would seem like a minor thing, but what it did was slightly enlarge the volume of material that the groove could hold. Again this seems like a minor thing. However—as I have said for years when I give technical presentations to the PGA of America or the sales force of a golf company—the grooves on the faces of golf clubs, when made to conform to the USGA specifications, serve mainly as a "rain gutter." By this I mean that the grooves are there to channel away dirt, grass, water, dew, and other types of foreign material that may get caught between the golf ball and the club face. The more volume a groove can hold, the better of a rain gutter it will be.

You have all seen a shot that you hit off the grass and leaves a small grass spot on the club face. Look closely and you'll see that some of the grass got pushed down into the grooves. This is grass that would have been directly between the ball and club face had the grooves not been there to help channel it away. Why is this important? It helps lessen the effect of a shot known as a "flyer," when a foreign material gets caught between the ball and the club face. The material does not allow the club face to grip the ball and put the required backspin on it. The backspin and ball dimples are what cause the ball to rise to its peak trajectory (the Bernoulli effect) and hold the line as it flies towards the target. A flyer, since it is hit with less backspin, will not reach its peak trajectory, flying lower and carrying farther. You may normally hit a number-five iron 160 yards, but with a flyer it may go 175 yards and over your target. (Of course, too much grass between the club face and the ball will just cause the ball to go a much shorter distance since the large amount of grass has absorbed much of the energy from your swing.) It was determined that the best club face for producing the greatest amount of ball spin was one with no grooves, like the slick tires on race cars. When the maximum amount of club face surface was in contact with the ball, the ball spun the best. Unfortunately, this only works if you play golf where there is no chance of any type of debris getting on the club face. Since we play golf outdoors in fields of grass and dirt, this is an impractical idea.

The rain gutter effect works well to help keep as much club face surface on the ball as legally possible. If a club designer begins to make the grooves larger than the USGA allows, then the groove channels away even more debris. If the club designer makes the grooves really large (well beyond the rules), the grooves themselves now begin to rough the ball surface and cause abnormal amounts of spin. Seventy to eighty years ago, when shafts were made of wood, club makers sold clubs that had grooves on the faces resembling a rippled potato chip. These clubs were called things like "the backspin mashie" and "deadstop niblick." These worked so well that the USGA decided that some of the skill was being taken away from the game and they outlawed them.

Nowadays, using conforming USGA grooves, some golf manufacturers are putting modern face coatings on the clubs to keep the face surface rough. All club faces have some type of surface blasting done prior to shipping them out to the golf retailer. Most of the faces are blasted with sand or aluminum oxide or the like. As you play golf with these clubs, the faces gradually get smoother. However, the golf clubs that are made with these face-coating techniques have a surface as rough as a new club, but this tough coating does not wear smooth as fast and you continue to get the grip on the ball for many more years.

Remember that it is not always just grooves that spin the ball. Rather it is a combination of a clean club face and clean grooves that allow the flat plane of the face to grip the maximum surface of the ball.

27

Don't Putt Rules Before Golfing Fun

David Grimes

Around of golf with President Clinton was sold in 1996 to a Virginia man for $76,000, or slightly less than you might have paid for a small sack of Jackie O's toenail clippings at Sotheby's. Clearly, the name "Clinton" does not yet give people the same warm, fuzzy feeling they get when they hear the name "Kennedy." Perhaps if Clinton spent more time secretly invading Cuba or hanging out with the Mafia and less time worrying about gays in the military, he could command a bigger fee for a round of golf.

Still, $76,000 is a substantial sum to pay for a round of golf, even in Sarasota at the peak of tourist season. You'd hope, for that kind of money, they'd at least throw in a complimentary sleeve of balls, a bag of tees, and maybe a coupon for a free hot dog and Coke after the round.

The price also seems high when you consider the very real

danger of standing anywhere near a U.S. president when he's got a golf club in his hands. Presidential golf is, at best, an inexact science and, at worst, an engine of mass destruction that leaves scores of bloodied victims in its wake.

President Clinton and former presidents Bush and Ford played together in a pro-am some time ago, and, by the time it was over, they just about needed a *M.A.S.H.* unit to repair all the spectators who had been on the receiving end of a presidential hook, slice, skank, or fizzer.

Some people have questioned the ethics of a sitting president auctioning off a round of golf, but nobody seems a bit concerned about the ethics of presidents whacking innocent civilians upside the head with errant drives, and charging them for the privilege.

From what I read in news reports, President Clinton also plays fast and loose with the Rules of Golf, which can be awfully frustrating if you've got a friendly wager going, as some golfers are known to do. Dropping $76,000 on a round of golf is one thing, but losing a $2 nassau to a guy who kicks his ball out from behind bushes is another thing entirely.

If somebody paid $76,000 to play a round of golf with me (step right up, folks; don't be shy), I would promise not to cheat unnecessarily and I would even agree to add up my score correctly, which is something I've occasionally had problems with in the past. We would play at the River Run Golf Links, one of the finest courses in the area built on top of an abandoned landfill. For $76,000, I would permit you to drop your ball, without penalty, from behind any refrigerators or washing machines that had popped out of the ground. Sinkholes, however, would be considered part of the course.

"I know you're the club's billiard champ, but I don't think this is covered in our rulebook!"

While I have the utmost respect for the Rules of Golf, some of the rules are just downright stupid and we should agree to ignore them before we tee off. Here are some examples:

If the golfer hits his ball into a sand trap, a water hazard, or a heavily wooded area that might be inhabited by snakes or other unsavory creatures, the golfer is entitled to declare the sand trap, water hazard, or wooded area a design flaw of the golf course and take free relief.

If a golfer misses a short putt, he is entitled to hit the putt over again as many times as it takes to make it and then record the

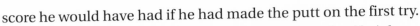

score he would have had if he had made the putt on the first try.

Any golfer who snickers at the aforementioned golfer's hapless putting will be assessed a penalty of two strokes and will also be required to buy the first round of drinks.

If a golfer moves a ball accidentally and no one sees him do it, there is no penalty. Also, dropping the ball nearer the hole is not only permitted, but almost always a good idea.

And, if you're playing golf with an ex-president, it might be a good idea to wear a football helmet.

28

Clubs with a Springlike Effect

Frank Fenton

The other day I got a letter from Dick Rugge, the Senior Technical Director at the United States Golf Association (USGA). Dick (formerly of Taylor Made), is tasked with making the rules for and testing golf clubs. There has been a lot of talk about these new clubs with thin, flexing faces that create a "trampoline" effect and produce incredibly long golf shots. Can this really be true? Does this actually happen? Didn't anyone think of this before? Well, the answer to all these questions is yes.

As you have undoubtedly heard, several golf companies are manufacturing metal wood drivers with very thin faces that the companies claim will flex and have a "springlike effect" on the golf ball, launching it into the stratosphere. This obviously worries the folks at the USGA. It is not causing as much concern with our friends across the ocean at the Royal & Ancient Golf

Club (R&A) in St. Andrews, Scotland. They decided, much to the USGA's consternation, that these clubs don't do all that much and that even if they do increase driving distance some small amount, it won't affect the way the game is played. The USGA feels quite differently. Dick Rugge's letter was about these clubs being tested for what the USGA calls the COR (coefficient of restitution) measurement test. As the USGA explains, this is a "ratio of velocities that measures the spring effect of drivers," which measures how fast a ball rebounds off the face of the golf head. This, they believe, will tell them if a club hits a ball too far.

The R&A has not yet come up with a test and may never bother to do so. In the past they did some testing of clubs at the University of Birmingham in England and felt that little was to be gained by further analyses. At that time they believed that the best way to test the clubs would be to use an ultrasonic measuring device to determine if the face, crown or sole of a club head is so thin that it will produce the trampoline effect. Since the R&A had decided to let things ride we saw, for a period of time, slightly different equipment being used by golfers in other parts of the world that are governed by R&A standards and not by USGA rules. American Tour players generally didn't feel that trying to break in a new driver for the British Open or other European Tour events was worth the trouble. They felt that the slight distance increase wasn't worth the potential of wayward tee shots with a driver that hadn't been tested under the heat of competition. As of January 1, 2003, the R&A goes by the same standards for COR as the USGA in "competitions for highly skilled players" (such as the British Open). Golfers under the rules of the R&A who were not participating in "competitions for highly skilled players" (such as your ordinary round of golf) may still use the "hot" drivers until the end of 2007, at which time the R&A and USGA will finally be in sync.

Through testing with golfers and the "Iron Byron" robotic machine, the USGA and R&A have determined that golfers can indeed hit farther with some of these clubs. How much? They are not saying, but some players claim an extra thirty yards, while others see only an additional eight to twelve yards. Most of the testing by golfers is far from scientific, but there is indeed an increase. Is this bad? For most players who hit the ball less than two hundred yards off the tee, it will add a few more yards and perhaps make the game more enjoyable to play. For Tour-quality players, the increase may be too much. Of course, if I hit the ball as hard as these Tour players, I might be more concerned with small cracks forming in the thin club faces and eventually causing off-line shots, or the face caving in entirely. This would not look good on TV.

Clubs like the Callaway ERC, Daiwa G3, Maruman Majesty, and—my favorite named club—Bridgestone's Break the Mode Joe Special were all on the USGA non-conforming list. Some of these clubs were selling for over $1,000 when they hit the marketplace. For this kind of money these things not only better hit the ball thirty yards farther, but they ought to get me a cold drink at the turn without my having to ask.

The interesting thing is that golf clubs with thin, flexing faces are not a new idea. I spoke with Pete Piotrowski not long ago and he was telling me about his early days in the golf club business at Wilson. Pete, a golf expert who has also worked for MacGregor, Hogan, Aldila, and Dave Pelz conducting research, remembers the Wilson Reflex clubs from the late 1970s. These clubs (and their sister model, the Hagan Ultra-Flex) were invented by Dan Campau. They had investment cast faces that were thin (for that time period) and did indeed flex and trampoline the ball to distances that, even then, the USGA felt was unfair. The prototype drivers had a cast metal insert installed in the center of the wooden face that flexed on impact to help propel the ball. Frank Thomas, former technical director at the USGA, didn't like this one bit and outlawed this driver and any other club with less than eighteen degrees loft.

Wilson made and sold a set of irons with a hot eighteen-degree driving iron, but the flexing-face woods never made it to market. The woods that were sold with these irons had standard laminated wooden heads with all the fancy decals to match the sizzling irons, but none of the springlike effect. As with most metal objects, if you flex them enough times hairline cracks begin to form, and they begin to fail. This is what happened to some of the Reflex irons until further research was done to figure out how to limit this cracking. By that time the craze of the flexing faces was diminishing and it would take over twenty years for the topic to become popular again.

29

How TV and Golf Magazines Favor the Large Golf Companies

Frank Fenton

Isn't it interesting that during a pro event on TV, the camera zooms in on a golf ball or a putter that is almost always one of two or three major brands? Why, it's plain to see that all pros use only these types of balls and equipment, right? Not so fast.

There is very good reason you may get this impression. The same few companies make it clear to the folks that broadcast golf events that they would be appreciative if their products got a little camera time. In years past, some cash in the hand of a cameraman would accomplish this, but not anymore. Nowadays, TV people go along with this to ensure that all those high-price ads targeted at the golden demographic of golf viewers are fully sold out week after week. An unsold minute of TV ad time can never be recouped. No sense in running those free public service announcements when companies are willing to pay good money for ad time. If a few close-ups of their product make the golf companies feel like they are getting a better deal, what's the harm? Well, the harm is that the public is getting a filtered view of what the pros really use.

Sure, big golf companies spend millions of dollars on Tour player endorsements and advertising. But the smaller, upstart companies that have a good product that the Tour players actually use will never get seen if this method persists. Lots of Tour players use a putter, wedge, driver, shaft, grip, and sometimes a ball that many golfers have never heard of. In golf, more so than in any other sport, players want to use what the pros use. There is an old saying in the golf equipment business that "what wins on Sunday sells on Monday." All golfers are convinced that the equipment a pro uses must be the key to the low rounds the pros shoot. After all, aren't you as talented as any pro? If only you didn't have that pesky job and you had more time to work on your game, you *know* that Tiger Woods and Phil Mickelson would be feeling the pinch of your taking all that prize money out of their pockets. Well, maybe not. But you do know that if you had all the little advantages that the pros do—getting the best and newest top-secret clubs and balls—you too could improve your game. This is why it's important to let golfers know what really goes on.

The way things are now, a smaller company has to rely on the accurate count of the Darrell Survey (which I discussed in an earlier chapter) to determine which pros are actually playing what type of products. Then, if the Darrell Survey found that their product is being used by the pros, it's up to the small companies to run expensive ads to inform the golfing public. I guess this is the American way, but if the media were really interested in informing the public of the truth, they would make an occasional attempt at showing some other products during the telecasts.

Golf magazines are not much better at enlightening the public when it comes to golf equipment. Most U.S. golf periodicals charge exorbitant prices for those big, full-page, four-color ads that catch your attention as you flip through your copy of the latest issue. These magazines are beginning to resemble the volume of a good-sized city's telephone book, and in some cases they have about as many actual golf articles as you would find in a phone book. I know that when conducting tests on equipment, a big advertiser never loses—or a least its results are never reported as a loss or deficiency, thanks to journalistic spin and omissions. I know that publications tell their readers that certain companies have huge usage on Tour, when the full story is that these big companies pay the players (including non-staff players to inflate the club count) a weekly stipend to use their products when most all the other companies do not pay such fees. I know that magazine editors and humor cartoonists must be very careful what they say and draw or risk the wrath of an unhappy advertiser. I've seen golf company executives make irate phone calls to publications threatening with (and in some cases following through) pulling upcoming advertising that the magazines may have already discounted for volume purchases to these bigger companies. You can bet that there is some serious back peddling on what is said or drawn in these journals, and that this sort of thing is frowned upon by the publication's upper management, who may face the loss of advertising revenue.

This does not happen worldwide, however. Golf magazines in Japan, for instance, are very dedicated to telling their readers what the pros really use. These publications take great delight in coming across a new putter or driver that their readers may not yet have heard of. They have the novel idea that they are actually in business to inform the golfing public rather than to regurgitate the same few brand names back to their readership over and over again.

Next time you are watching a golf tournament on TV or reading your favorite golf publication, keep in mind that the things made obvious to you may be slightly distorted in their presentation. Look closer at your TV screen and the blurry photos in the magazines to get a glimpse of what the pros might really be playing. How else are you going to improve your game? Hitting a bucket of balls faithfully each week hasn't helped. It's got to be the equipment.

30

Thai Prime Minister Has Golf All Shook Up

David Grimes

These days, it seems that every professional athlete worth his or her appearance fee consults with a sports psychologist.

The psychologists try to help the athlete relax, visualize success, and play to the best of his or her abilities. Thailand's Prime Minister Thaksin Shinawatra thinks he's found a way to accomplish the same thing for a lot less money: When he plays golf, he sings Elvis songs to keep himself calm. Elvis' hit, "Love Me Tender," is especially relaxing, he says.

I do not know how good a singer the prime minister is, or how the other members of his foursome like having him burst into song in the middle of their backswings. (There is also the matter of how well the Mississippi-born Elvis' lyrics translate into Thai, but let us set that aside for the moment.)

Golf, unlike many other sports, is played at a leisurely pace, giving the mind plenty of time to wander into areas that are not always conducive to good play. An Elvis fan like the prime minister could easily find himself humming tunes that could hurt his game rather than help it.

"Don't Be Cruel" is an example of an Elvis song that the prime minister would probably do well to block from his mind. He does not need to be reminded that golf is a cruel and unforgiving game and that begging for mercy usually only makes matters worse.

Another Elvis song the prime minister shouldn't think about is "And the Grass Won't Pay No Mind." Bad bounces are part of the game and singing about them is not likely to make one feel better about a shot that took a wicked right-angle hop into a lake, trap, or snake-infested bog.

Positive thinking is as important in golf as in any other sport, which is why the prime minister should definitely refrain from singing the Elvis song, "Don't." If the prime minister really wants to tie himself up in knots and shoot the worst score of his life, he might follow up "Don't" with "Paralyzed." That is what happens when a golfer gets a couple dozen swing thoughts swirling through his head at the same time, usually the result of reading too many instructional golf articles.

"I'm Left, You're Right, She's Gone" is a common refrain of golfers who have trouble finding the middle of the fairway and lose a lot of golf balls. It is also another Elvis song the prime minister would do well to let go.

Even the best golfers hit a bad shot now and then, but that is no reason for the prime minister to add the Elvis song "Trouble" to his playlist. If he does, depending on how much trouble he finds, the prime minister may find himself singing "Fool, Fool, Fool" and actually feeling like one.

By this time, it's likely that the prime minister's head is

swirling with unsettling Elvis songs. If that is the case, the prime minister should grasp his scorecard firmly in both hands and take Elvis' musical advice: "Rip It Up."

31

Cannes

Frank Fenton

As I watched the final few holes of the 2000 Wales Open on the Golf Channel, I saw my old acquaintance, Steen Tinning from Denmark, break through for his first European PGA Tour win. In my golf business travels I get to go to some truly interesting places. I had met Steen a few years back when I attended the Cannes Open in France to work with some of the Spalding Tour players. This event was played at the Royal Mouglins Golf Club in the beautiful hills above the Mediterranean seaport of Cannes.

I had been to many other countries in my golf travels, but never to France. I remember that I had been traveling quite a bit and when the folks at Spalding asked me to attend another event, this time over Easter weekend, I at first declined. I was a member of seven different frequent flyers clubs and the thought of earning more miles didn't excite me. But when they said that I was really needed to help fit some of the European staff players with clubs and that we would be staying at one of the best hotels on the French Riviera, I gave in.

My traveling companion was Jacques Hetrick, who was director of communications at Spalding. Jacques (who was American and we called "Jock") had one of the best jobs in the sports business. Whenever one of the Spalding staff players needed something, he took care of it. If basketball greats Larry Bird or Dr. J needed to be picked up at the airport in a limo, Jacques was there. He flew in a helicopter with Greg Norman over Italy to inspect the latest golf course design and made sure that Roger Clemens had everything he needed to pitch his way to another Cy Young Award. Jacques knew how to travel. Whenever we checked into a hotel he was very particular about the details. He expected, and usually received, good service.

After we had taken a red-eye out of New York to Paris and then on to Nice, we were quite tired. We were eventually picked up by an associate of the European Spalding division, a Swedish TV announcer whose name now escapes me. He was a nice fellow, but his tardiness and our all-night flight left Jacques in no mood to exchange pleasantries. As we drove from Nice to our hotel I began to see some sights that looked familiar. We went right past the theater that hosts the Cannes Film Festival. We continued a short distance more and pulled up to the front of the Intercontinental Hotel, directly on the main road facing the Mediterranean Sea. I mean the beach was right out of the front entrance. Off in the distance, I was told, Monaco stood around the mountains to the east, near the Italian border. This was spectacular. The hotel looked like a big white wedding cake with all its ornate architecture. Every time they show bits of the

Cannes Film Festival, you are sure to see this marvelous hotel, with all the movie stars hanging around the front or on the patio sipping drinks with friends. "This must be costing Spalding a fortune," I thought.

When Jacques and I checked in, I noticed that the Swedish TV guy spoke with the desk clerk. Jacques said nothing as he signed the register. I got my key and as we went up to our rooms we agreed to get some quick rest, clean up, and meet in the lobby for a dinner engagement with some of the Tour players. My room was okay, perhaps a little small and old, but I had traveled to England and Scotland before and thought that this was the norm for European hotel rooms. My window overlooked a courtyard that housed part of the employee car park. Nothing too interesting. Later, when I went down to see Jacques at his room, I realized that he had been assigned a much superior room. Everything was brand new. It was larger and brighter and it overlooked the patio bar area, where nice-looking people could enjoy the sunshine. Obviously, having the Swedish TV guy talk to the check-in clerk and being named "Jacques" in France had help secure this room. Now I knew why Jacques was so subdued during check-in. He didn't want them to hear his American accent but allowed them to think he was a countryman. I had to laugh, as this ruse obviously had worked. Jacques and I were told that the rooms were over $400 per night, but days later when we checked out we were charged the European PGA Tour rate of only $78. It pays to know the right people in Cannes.

At dinner that evening, we were joined by the Swedish TV guy and several of the Spalding staff players, Steen Tinning, and Fredrik Lindgren, and Mats Lanner from Sweden. In the U.S. I could take or leave French cooking, but I'm going to tell you that everything they served us in Cannes was incredible. As we engaged in dinner conversation, some in English, some in French, some in Swedish, Fredrik and I began discussing golf clubs and the Hogan Apex BH88 came up. I told him of my involvement in the design of this club and how, before its introduction, I had tested it in various areas of the U.S. with many different players to get their opinions on its performance. He said that he had test hit some of the early prototypes while he was attending college in America in Jacksonville, Florida. Suddenly, we looked at each other, simultaneously realizing that we already knew each other from those days of testing years before. Here I was sitting in a restaurant in France, talking with a Swedish player that I had met as a test subject in Florida while developing golf clubs in the U.S. for a Texas company. What a small world.

The next day we were at the practice range of the Royal Mouglins Golf Club and I got a chance to see some of the European players up close. I had heard some of their names before, but since few of them came to the U.S., I didn't know much about their games. Most of them had what was considered very "stylish" swings and mannerisms. They dressed well and had fluid, if not powerful, swings. It almost seemed like it was more important to some of them to look good, even if they shot continuous rounds in the mid–to low seventies. Compared to the U.S. PGA Tour as a group I felt that they didn't have a lot of depth. There were, however, a few players with strong impressive swings. I stood next to a fellow who I had not heard much about except for his unusual name, Vijay Singh. He was taller than I had thought, with a full, flowing, potent swing. He easily beat balls to the end of the range. I remember how long he stayed on the range, never seeming to tire from all the practicing. "This guy is gonna win something big some day," I thought.

It took him a few years, but Vijay won the PGA Championship and then the 2000 Masters. If he had been a better putter you would have heard about him much sooner. I also thought that my friend Steen Tinning was a powerful hitter who seemed to have a good game. I watched for years as he toiled on the Euro circuit without any luck. Recently he has been working with a sports psychologist who must have helped him realize what a great ball striker he is. It finally paid off, that week in Wales. Good for him.

32

Iron Byron

Frank Fenton

I was watching TV the other day and another one of those slick infomercials came on touting a new club that would cure all the ills of my game. "More distance, more accuracy, higher trajectory with incredible roll." The poor golf course wouldn't have a chance. I would finally be able to shoot that fifty-nine that I'd been dreaming of.

To prove their point they show a test of their new golf club on the robotic-swinging Iron Byron. Now, I've known old Iron Byron (IB) personally for nearly seventeen years, and I can tell you one thing for sure. He aims to please. If you set up IB to make your new test club look good, he'll do a fine job. Just a slight tweak here and a small adjustment there, and your new test club will be king of the hill. IB will do exactly what you set him up to do. Is this really a test?

To be fair, the robotic hitting machine that we often call Iron

Byron is a great piece of test equipment if we are brave enough to accept the pure data as it comes forth. These types of machines will accurately reproduce a certain golf swing—anything from a perfect, powerful, Tour-player quality swing to a weak, open face duck slice—for as many hits as we require to put together some meaningful statistical data. You can't do that with humans.

The setup involved in getting an IB ready to hit test shots can take from thirty minutes to two hours to prepare for only one type of shot. Thank God we don't have to play behind IB on the weekends! When the USGA was using their IB to conduct ball testing it would take up to two weeks for them to be satisfied that all was running correctly. Just about then, a shaft would break or a nut would work loose and the setup would start all over again.

When you witness an IB test in person you marvel at the intricate multi-motion swing that this machine will repeat. You also gain true respect for the scratch golfer and Tour player who are able to duplicate this shot in a matter of seconds. The live golfer will factor in the uneven stance, wind, lie of the ball, and the particular golf club he is about to swing. And then, as if by some divine gift, he will whip off a shot that IB can only dream of. People can play this game!

Anyway, back to the Iron Byron tests seen in these infomercials. To create a truly fair contest, all the test clubs should be the same length, lie, loft, face angle, CG, overall weight, swing weight, and shaft type. Since competitors almost never sell exactly the same type of club (what would be the point of coming out with a new club if it were exactly the same as the others on the market?), the test is usually biased toward the characteristics of the new club during the machine set up. With this inclination in place, the edge is given to the new test club.

Also, you will seldom see an "independent testing group" charge their client to lose a test. I'm not saying that all these people are cheating. I'm just pointing out that there are certain ways that new clubs in expensive infomercials can win a test under certain conditions. Does this mean that these new wonder clubs are right for you? Maybe, maybe not. That is why I am a big proponent of the live golfer test. Live golfer tests involve real people of known golfing ability (whether it is Tour-caliber or a one hundred shooter) who actually go out and play with or hit range balls with the test product. The data you gather can be statistically meaningful if you have enough shots that have been accurately recorded, but usually you just go by the comments and feelings of the golfers who participate. After all, it's live golfers who buy all this stuff. What they think, feel, and say is more important than stacks of data from a machine. New clubs might as well be tested by real people rather than Iron Byron. Come to think of it, IB never pays for the drinks after the round, either. What do you expect from a robot?

33

A Divot off the Old Green

David Grimes

I think I reacted the way any parent would after seeing Tiger Woods tearfully embrace his father following his emotional victory in the 1997 Masters golf tournament.

"Son," I said to the eleven-year-old, "it's time to get your worthless butt out to the driving range."

From what I've read, Tiger Woods hit his first golf ball while still a fetus and was walloping four-hundred-yard drives and regularly beating Jack Nicklaus before he was out of diapers.

I'm just guessing, but I bet by the time he was eleven, Tiger had his own agent, his own corporate jet, and was flying back and forth to Washington, D.C., on weekends for overnights in the Lincoln bedroom.

The talents of my own eleven-year-old, on the other hand, basically consist of getting to level four in Super Mario Bros. and having an ability to make bathroom noises by squeezing his hand in his armpit.

"And please, Dear Lord, have daddy get a hole in one tomorrow, the day we get our report cards!"

Despite these accomplishments, it seemed to me that I would have a better chance of retiring comfortably if my son were a world-class professional golfer with a $60-million endorsement deal with Nike rather than a person who collects spare change by standing around on street corners making armpit noises.

Tiger Woods' father, Earl, gave Tiger most of his early golf instruction, so I figured that was the way to go if I wanted my son to be pulling down millions before he started sixth grade.

The day was bright and sunny as we pulled into the parking lot of a local public course. I could tell that the sight of the wide, green fairways, sparkling lakes, and abundant wildlife was fueling the boy's excitement.

"Ohhhh!" he said. "There's a snack bar! Can I get a Coke and a Milky Way?" After our snack, I bought two large buckets of balls and we headed to the driving range.

"The first thing you should know," I began, "is that golf is a very simple game. All you've got to remember is keep your left arm straight, right arm bent, chin pointed behind the ball, knees flexed, weight on the balls of your feet, shoulders and toes parallel to the target line, grip pressure light, shoulders relaxed, and wallet tucked into your left hip pocket at a sixty-degree angle to your spine. Now you're ready to start your backswing."

During the time it took me to complete this first part of my dissertation, my son had hit half a dozen golf balls and seemed to be enjoying himself immensely.

"To start the backswing," I continued, "push the club head back slow and low without breaking your wrists and keeping the back of the left hand square to the target line. While Hogan espoused pronating the left wrist, most modern instructors recommend that you let your hands open of their own accord, synchronized, of course, with the coiling of the shoulders and hips."

I noticed that my son had now polished off half a bucket of balls and was engaged in a driving contest with another youngster who had been brought to the driving range by his dad.

Some parents, I thought to myself. Probably thinks his kid is going to be the next Tiger Woods. Hey, pal. Get a life, why don't you?

"At the top of the backswing," I resumed, "take care that the shaft is pointed down the target line and that you have loaded anywhere between 73.5 and 77.2 percent of your weight onto your right side, checking to make sure your right knee has remained in the address position."

When I looked up next, my son and the other boy had quit hitting balls and were engaged in a spirited conversation about Super Mario Bros.

That evening, to his glee, he conquered level five.

34

St. Andrews

Frank Fenton

O n one of my trips overseas to meet with some of the European PGA Tour players at the British Open, I got the opportunity to visit the town of St. Andrews in Scotland. The Open Championship was being held at Royal Troon, which was, and still is, on the other side of the country from St. Andrews, so there was a chance to play the Old Course that particular year.

Through my connections in the golf business I had made advance arrangements with a gentleman named George Wilson, who at that time was the Deputy Secretary of the Royal and Ancient Golf Club of St. Andrews. The R&A is headquartered in the fine old building that you see by the first tee and eighteenth green of the Old Course in all the photos and paintings. The Old Course is situated on the North Sea by the Firth of Forth. People have been playing golf on these links for over five hundred years. Mr. Wilson was nice enough to offer me a tour of the R&A clubhouse and to enter my name in the lottery system that the town of St. Andrews used to determine who would be granted a tee time on the Old Course. This was a few years ago. Now, I understand, it is very difficult to get on the Old Course without paying a princely sum of cash. I think that at that time I paid around 35 pounds, or about $53 at the time.

When I reached Edinburgh, the capital of Scotland, I telephoned Mr. Wilson to find out when my tee time was. He told me that the lottery had not yet been held for that day and I would have to take a chance that I would get a time assigned on the day that I had wished to play. I had come a long way and I knew that if I missed out playing during this trip I would not get a chance to play the Old Course anytime in the near future.

The day I had planned to play arrived. We had nice weather as we set off for the Old Course. A good sign. I wasn't really sure how to get to the R&A Golf Club, or, for that matter, the town of St. Andrews. With my wife Kathy, acting as navigator, I drove our rental car along the country roads that led to the town. When we reached the outskirts of St. Andrews, she told me that we had no further directions and asked how I would find the golf links. I don't exactly know how to explain it, but I was drawn to the course by some feeling that I had been there before. I can only guess that since I had been watching golf tournaments being played on the Old Course on TV since I was a kid, I must have figured if I kept going down to the sea I would find it. I followed this feeling and ended right in the car park at the R&A. Another good sign.

I went inside and met the club manager, who confirmed my tee time and asked me to put on a jacket and tie. He then said that I could tour the old clubhouse. Unfortunately, at that time, no women were allowed inside. My wife took this well and set out to see the St. Andrews Cathedral and the castle ruins and to check out the deals at the woolen shops. We made plans to meet after my round of golf was complete.

I was paired with one of the members of the R&A and two Americans. I had brought my immense, tour-size staff bag packed with a rain suit, an extra pair of shoes, extra balls, and a full set of clubs. When I approached the caddie master on the first tee, the caddies who were there literally scattered. I was told that no caddies were available. This couldn't be true! What were all these caddies here for? He told me that they had either already been out and were done for the day, or they were there waiting for their golfers to show up to play. I felt that the real reason was the intimidating size of my staff bag. I knew there was no way I could enjoy the round and carry that heavy bag. I quickly ran back up to the R&A clubhouse and asked if I could leave some of my things there while I played. I hastily jettisoned rain gear, extra shoes, several clubs, and whatever else I felt I could do without that day. The club manager asked if I would like to borrow his trolley as he pointed to an old pull cart in the corner. Now, I hadn't pulled my clubs since I was 15 years old. This just wasn't done with the really cool tour-style staff bag that I had. I thought for a millisecond and gladly accepted. I knew that I was not going to carry that huge bag all the way around the Old Course.

We finally got to the first tee and even though I was nervous, I hit a solid drive down the fairway, just short of the burn in front of number one green. As I look back on this, I realize how much trouble there was. The burn comes quickly into play on the left and right if you pull or push your tee shot, and the beach guards the far right side. I am not sure that a well-hit driver is the play from this tee. I won't bore you with a shot-by-shot recollection of my round, but a few things are worth recounting.

As we played the first couple of holes I asked the R&A member we were playing with for some distance help. He told me that he didn't really know the distances. This can't be, I thought. "You did say that you are a member here, right?" He assured me that he was and that he had been playing the Old Course for many years. They just don't go by yardage much there. The weather conditions change so dramatically from day to day (sometimes from minute to minute) that they pretty much size up a shot by eye and past experience and fire away. In the U.S. we get so used to playing by yardage and flying the ball to the target that we forget how to feel a shot and stroke it to the green. The sunny sky, firm ground, and slight wind (for Scotland) made me feel like I was playing back in Fort Worth, Texas, so that's what I kept in mind the rest of the day.

As I learned a little more about running or bouncing the ball along the firm, springy turf, I began to have quite a grand time playing golf this way. I had my swings at hacking the ball out of the heather and gorse (the thick, shrublike rough) and I even drove one of the short par fours in one. Two putted for my birdie. This great feat impressed the caddies in the group behind us. (I'll bet they were sorry that they didn't get to carry my bag then.) I got to play out of Hell bunker on the long par five fourteenth and hit over the Old Course Hotel sign on the number seventeen Road Hole. On the number eighteen tee I pulled my drive off to the left by number one fairway.

When we left the tee I turned to walk right. "Where are you

going?" the R&A member called after me. I told him, "I didn't come all this way to miss walking over the Swilken Burn bridge. Who knows when I'll be back." This is the same bridge that the world's greatest golfers have traversed over for hundreds of years. You might remember it from seeing the photo of Arnold Palmer waving good-bye to the crowds as he played in his last British Open. I hit my approach shot onto the green as the crowd that gathers each day applauded. These people cherish the game of golf and even my minor shot was appreciated. What a glorious day. This was one of those days that confirms your reasons for playing the game. It was not only a challenge, but great fun.

If you ever get the chance to play the Old Course, or for that matter, anywhere in Scotland, jump on it. This is where the game, as we know it, started. You'll remember it for the rest of your life.

35

Gene Sarazen

Frank Fenton

One of my first jobs in the golf business was as a golf professional at the Bethesda Country Club outside of Washington, D.C., in the late 1970s. Jim Folks was and still is the head golf professional and has done a fine job there for many years. There are some famous clubs in that area such as the Congressional C.C., where the 1964 and 1997 U.S. Open and 1976 PGA Championship were played, and the TPC at Avenel, where the PGA Tour event is played each year. Old line classic courses like Burning Tree, Chevy Chase Club, and Columbia C.C. are just down the road. With this much great golf in the immediate area, we saw some interesting people come through there from time to time.

I sometimes worked on Mondays, after a long, hard weekend. The club was technically closed for at least half the day, and the pace was slower compared to the rest of the week. The grounds crew had time then to attend to the course after all the play earlier in the week and on the weekend. I had the morning to get the shop in shape or repair clubs. One morning I was in the shop working by myself, and there was a knock at the locked door. It was a guest of one of our members who was a little early for his game that afternoon. Since the locker room was also closed that day, he asked if he could come in and change into his golf shoes. I let him in. As he got ready to play, a transformation took place. He rolled up his pant legs and put some elastic bands just below his knees to hold the end of the trousers. He then rolled down the excess pant leg length and was suddenly wearing knickers or, as he called them, "plus fours." Remember, this is years before Payne Stewart made this type of pants popular again, so it was extremely rare to see anyone wearing such things. Next, he put on his black and white, two-tone wing-tip golf shoes, and finally, his bucket-style golf hat. When he stood up I said to myself, "Who is this guy?" Then it hit me. It was Gene Sarazen! The "Squire." An actual, honest-to-God legend right here in my shop! Ever since I was a kid I remembered watching the old Shell's Wonderful World of Golf television show and seeing this fellow go all over the world to comment on matches between the best golfers of the day. Some of these old programs are now being shown on the Golf Channel and are well worth watching.

For those of you who may be a little rusty on your golf history, let me remind you of some of Gene Sarazen's accomplishments. His first victory was the Southern Open in 1922. He followed that quickly with the 1922 U.S. Open, where he beat Bobby Jones, and the 1922 PGA Championship. Not a bad year for someone only twenty years old. In 1923, he won the PGA again. He captured the U.S. Open a second time in 1932.

Just before he was to make the long trip by sea to Great Britain for the 1932 British Open, he was down in Florida working on his game. Sarazen knew that he would need something special to get out of all those steep bunkers that are so prevalent on British Open links. He had been flying with Howard Hughes in Hughes' plane and noticed how pulling the front end of the plane up (rear down) made the plane climb. He then figured that the rear of the sole of a golf club would not dig in the sand if the sole was lower toward the rear. This effect is what would come to be known among club designers as "bounce" years later. With this idea in mind, he bought up all the solder he could locate in New Port Richey, Florida, and had Wilson Sporting Goods send him some of the standard thin-soled niblicks of the day. He went to work and created what was to become the precursor of all modern-day sand wedges. He took this club with him to the British Open, being careful to keep the club upside down in his bag so no one would see his invention. He used the new weapon like a wizard and won that year's British Open Championship.

He claimed his third PGA in 1933. The first Masters was played in 1934, but Sarazen had a previous commitment and couldn't play. The next year, 1935, playing in his first Masters, he made his famous double eagle on number fifteen, the par five, and won the Masters. He was the first golfer to win all the modern day majors, the "Grand Slam."

What a treat it was for me to talk with Mr. Sarazen. During his many visits we chatted about new club designs and his famous, flat-sided "reminder grip," which Wilson offered on its clubs for so many years. He was still using this type of grip on his clubs at the time. He would have his clubs gripped with a standard round rubber grip and then he would take a sharp knife and carve down the left front side of the grip so his left hand would fit on to the flat he had made. I remember that we discussed putter designs and as we reviewed some of the popular modern heel-toe cavity back designs, he said that the harsh angled necks looked like "bad plumbing" to him.

Wilson had a wedge out at the time with "Gene Sarazen" on it. He said that, although it was a good utility wedge (very rounded sole with little bounce), it was not like the one he used. At that time he had one of the "Sandy Andy" wedges with a lot of bounce (not the old aluminum head Sandy Andy with a radius sole from the 1920s, but rather the steel-head one from the early 1960s). It was great fun to watch him pop shots out of the bunker by the ninth green on the Bethesda course. Even though he must have been seventy-five or seventy-six at the time and didn't hit the ball very far, he would just finesse the ball around the course and shoot scores that I wish I could have shot. I recall one day he had to "feather" a driver to the long par three ninth, but he still wound up scoring a sixty-nine for the round.

I always looked forward to those early Monday mornings. What incredible fortune I had to actually talk golf with one of the all-time greats of the game.

36

Letters to the Editor

David Grimes

Dear Editor:

I was playing with my usual foursome at the club the other day when my partner, Harry, suffered a heart attack and fell to the ground on the fifth green. This was unfortunate timing on Harry's part as he had a five-foot uphill birdie putt that would have put us up three-and-one on the $5 nassau. I asked Harry if he wouldn't mind putting out before we called the ambulance, but all he did was lie there clutching his chest and making this disgusting gurgling sound. I contended that since Harry was unable to putt for himself, I should be allowed to putt out for him, but my opponents said that would be a clear violation of Article Six, Section 3.2, Paragraph F, Clause 187xd.3a of the Rules of Golf that classifies an incapacitated golfer as a loose impediment from which you are entitled to a two club-length drop, no closer to the hole. Since Harry could not putt out for himself, they claimed we forfeited the hole, putting us one up on the original bet and one down on the press. My question to you is this: Do you think I can get more distance with one of those new, big-headed titanium drivers?

Confused in Catonsville

Dear Confused:

Absolutely. But please do not stop with titanium. There are many, many other metals and alloys available to golfers willing to sacrifice their kids' college fund for a few extra yards off the tee. Be advised that some of these alloys are a trifle—how shall we say?—unstable, particularly the Mushroom Cloud 2000 that is made by mixing titanium with weapons-grade plutonium. But, hey, what are a few radiation burns compared to the thrill of reaching the par fives in two? Go get 'em, tiger!

Dear Editor:

I am a young, successful stockbroker who recently took up golf. Although I love to play, it's important that I stay in touch with my office, so I bring my cell phone with me to the course. The problem is my playing companions get annoyed when my phone rings, even though I seldom make or receive more than 10 or 15 calls per round. I say it's not my problem that these people are underachieving losers who don't appreciate how important I am and how our nation's entire financial system would collapse if I don't make a margin call when they're standing over a 3-foot putt. How can I set them straight?

Busy in Bradenton

Dear Busy:

Your playing partners certainly sound like a bunch of prissy, insensitive clods who are always complaining about something. It has nothing to do with you; these people would whine if a bird chirped or a car alarm went off in the middle of their backswing. We suggest you find some different people to play with, preferably people who share your view that the golf course is just an extension of the office, only with more trees.

Dear Editor:

As is so often the case these days, the golf course that I play winds through a subdivision. Some of the homes are in the "line of fire" and suffer torn pool screens, broken windows, and other damage from errant golf balls. I had the misfortune of badly slicing my drive on the par four sixth hole last weekend and watched helplessly as my ball crashed through the den window of my friend, Jim. I went to apologize only to find that my ball had struck Jim in the side of the head while he was working on his computer, causing him to spill his coffee. Jim was out cold, but the ball was sitting not too badly on his desk in about a quarter of an inch of lukewarm Maxwell House. I had a clear chip through his window back to the fairway, from where I figured I could make five and possibly tie the hole. Would you recommend a lob wedge or an eight iron for this shot?

Perplexed in Pawtucket

Dear Perplexed:

We would recommend a less-lofted club, such as a six iron or possibly a five. Your lob wedge would probably "bounce" off the hard surface of the desk. (If the ball had come to rest on

Jim's mouse pad, you probably could have played the shot with an eight or nine iron.) You didn't specify what kind of stance you had or whether Jim's body would restrict your backswing. Assuming everything is normal, we would suggest playing a low punch shot through the broken window, keeping your weight forward, the ball back in your stance and your hands well ahead of the ball. Stay down on the shot (some glass may fly back at you) and keep your follow-through short so as to avoid any additional damage to Jim's floor lamp, walls, or bookcases. After you play the shot, it would be a nice gesture to mop up the spilled coffee since Jim is a personal friend of yours. You will probably find some clean towels in his bathroom.

Index

NOTE: This index refers to chapters by Frank Fenton

If you enjoyed reading this book, here are some other Pineapple Press titles you might enjoy as well. To request our complete catalog or to place an order, write to Pineapple Press, P.O. Box 3889, Sarasota, Florida 34230, or call 1–800-PINEAPL (746–3275). Or visit our website at www.pineapplepress.com.

52 Great Florida Golf Getaways by Ed Schmidt, Jr. From the white sand bunkers of the Panhandle to the palmetto-framed fairways of Miami, this book offers Florida's best places to tee up—including information on courses, strategies, golf schools, and course architects. ISBN 1–56164–260–6 (pb)

Everglades Lawmen by James T. Huffstodt. Ride along on an airboat as it whooshes through sawgrass marshes. Hitch a ride on a track as it chugs and grumbles over the Glades' rough terrain. Meet the men and women who have dedicated their lives to protecting the wildlife and natural resources in the only Everglades on earth. ISBN 1–56164–192–8 (pb)

Florida Fun Facts by Eliot Kleinberg. At last—a collection of every fact, large and small, that you need to know about Florida. Answers to questions like these: What's bigger, Lake Okeechobee or Rhode Island? What's wrong with Citrus County's name? And hundreds more! ISBN 1–56164–068–9 (pb)

Florida Place Names by Allen Morris. This book paints a rich historical portrait of the state and reveals the dreams, memories, and sense of humor of the people who have called Florida home over the years. ISBN 1–56164–084–0 (hb)

The Sunshine State Almanac and Book of Florida-Related Stuff by Phil Philcox and Beverly Boe. Chock-full of statistics, recipes, and photos, this handy reference is a veritable cornucopia of helpful and just plain fascinating stuff! Includes a long list of what's going on around Florida every month of the year. ISBN 1–56164–178–2 (pb)

Tourists, Retirees, and Other Reasons to Stay in Bed by David Grimes. David Grimes began writing his humor column for the *Sarasota Herald Tribune* in 1985, when it became clear that he had no talent for other, more useful jobs at the paper. He has gleaned a lifetime of wisdom from his 25 years as a Florida resident and offers us his sage advice on topics such as "Granny Sweat Boosts Health," "Let the Feds Cut Your Grass," "How to Increase Holiday Bickering," and much more. ISBN 1–56164–207X (pb)

You Got Me!—Florida by Rob Lloyd. Get an insider's grasp of the Sunshine State. Meticulously researched, this is a reference that will tickle your funny bone and tease your brain at the same time. ISBN 1–56164–178–2 (pb)